DISCOVERING WHO I AM

FROM GOD'S PERSPECTIVE

A PARENT GUIDED DEVOTIONAL

FOR KIDS, AGES 6-12

AUTHORED BY

MELISSA ADKISON

EDITED BY CARRIE JOHNSON

DISCOVERING WHO I AM
FROM GOD'S PERSPECTIVE

ISBN: 978-0-578-51643-1

APPLYING FAITH

CONTENTS

INTRODUCTION

A parent's perspective is different than God's perspective. As a mother, I know what I want for my child. When my daughter was born, I gave her a special name. With parental help, she learned to recognize and say her name. As she grew, she understood the specific role and relationship she had within the family unit and community. But, do we as parents, truly teach our children who they are from God's perspective? From His perspective, our children are much more than our sons, daughters, siblings, or grandchildren, etc. Each child is handpicked by God before the creation of the world. Unique qualities and a one of a kind personality is given to each child to aid in performing God's will. God has a specific, good, and divine plan for every child!

1

My prayer is that each child who follows this devotional will:

> ➢ gain a true understanding of one's self,

> ➢ grasp the reality of God's unending and unconditional love,

> ➢ develop a solid foundation for a lifelong relationship with God.

HOW TO USE THIS DEVOTIONAL

The instructions for this devotional are really quite simple. All you need is about 10-15 minutes with your child each day. First, begin with your child reading the daily confession and memory scripture or your child may repeat after you as you read the daily confession and memory scripture. Next, either you or your child should read aloud the short story for the day and discuss the questions and thoughts to consider that follow each story. Finally, all of the daily devotions conclude with a simple prayer for your child to pray.

Reminder: Allow 10-15 minutes to complete the following steps;

> ➤ Read the daily confession

> ➤ Read the memory scripture

> ➤ Read the story, questions, and thoughts to consider

> ➤ Pray.

In order to commit a piece of information to memory, we need to be continuously reminded of that information. Because of this need, each memory scripture is repeated for 7 daily devotionals. The daily confession is also repeated for 7 days; however, you will notice that all new daily confessions include the previous confessions as well. In other words, the daily confession starts off with a simple sentence, and each week a new sentence is added to the confession. This process will result in the memory scriptures and daily confessions becoming firmly rooted in your child's heart and mind by the time he or she finishes the devotional.

PARENT'S PRAYER

Dear heavenly Father,

Thank You for giving me my child, who is a blessing from You. Please give me divine wisdom on how to best use this devotional with my child. According to James 1:5, You generously give wisdom to all who ask. I thank You in advance for giving me abundant wisdom. In Jesus' name, I pray. Amen.

DAY 1

DAILY CONFESSION

God wonderfully made me, and I am precious[1] to Him.

MEMORY SCRIPTURE

I praise you because I am fearfully and wonderfully made; your works are wonderful, I know that full well. Psalm 139:14

ETHAN'S STORY

Ethan angrily stared at his face in the bathroom mirror. *Why did I have to be born this way?* he thought as his eyes scanned over his birthmark. There was no way to disguise the blotchy purplish-red discoloration. It began near the inside of his left eye, gradually became wider as it ran along his left cheekbone, and ended near his hairline. The longer he stared at his face, the more he disliked himself.

"You are supposed to be washing your hands for dinner, Ethan," his mom scolded as she neared the silent bathroom. Ethan quickly turned his focus from the mirror and began soaping his hands. His mom knocked gently on the partially open door and immediately poked her head into the bathroom. She silently studied Ethan's expression. "Hey, are you okay?" she tenderly asked.

"I'm fine. I will be done in a minute," he sharply stated.

She paused before she responded, "Honey, it seems like something is upsetting you. You know, you can talk to me about anything."

Ethan attempted to focus on washing his hands. He was not in the mood for a conversation with his mom. Although, before his mind could talk himself out of it, he blurted, "I hate my face!"

Fighting back tears, Ethan's mom replied, "I have no idea what it is like to have a birthmark on my face. I can't imagine how that affects the way you see yourself or how you feel about yourself. Nonetheless, there are some things that I *do know*. For one, I love you more than you can imagine. When I look at you, I see a handsome young man who stole my heart from the moment he was born. I love everything about you, including your face, and God's love for you is even bigger than my love for you. I wish you could see yourself the way that I see you and the way that God sees you."

QUESTIONS TO DISCUSS

- ➢ Considering today's memory scripture, what does the Bible say about Ethan's face?
- ➢ How do you think God views your appearance?

THOUGHTS TO CONSIDER

You were made by God. The memory scripture teaches that you were *wonderfully* made, and you are precious to God. According to oxforddictionaries.com, precious means of great value; not to be wasted or treated carelessly.

Your entire body, from your hair and face, to your arms and waist, to your legs and feet, are all wonderful and precious to God. He cares for every part of your body. And, it doesn't stop there. He thinks your mind and soul are wonderful and precious too! Take time to think about how you view yourself, and correct any negative thoughts you might have had.

PRAYER

Dear heavenly Father,

Thank You for showing me that You wonderfully made me, and that I am precious to You. Please help me to recognize any thoughts I have about myself that do not line up with your truth. I am grateful that You think I am precious. Thank You for your amazing love. In Jesus' name, I pray. Amen.

DAY 2

DAILY CONFESSION

God wonderfully made me, and I am precious[1] to Him.

MEMORY SCRIPTURE

I praise you because I am fearfully and wonderfully made; your works are wonderful, I know that full well. Psalm 139:14

ETHAN'S STORY CONTINUED

"This treehouse kit has most of the features you want, Ethan. It has a rope ladder, a slide and a rock wall. It doesn't have a telescope, but I could easily buy that separately and attach it to the included window ledge," Ethan's dad stated.

"That's awesome!" Ethan exclaimed.

His dad smiled and chuckled to himself. He was almost as excited about working on a project with his son as Ethan was about having his own treehouse. Ethan held the cart in place as the hardware store employee assisted his dad with loading the large kit onto the store cart. Ethan and his dad chatted about the new endeavor all the way to the checkout line, where they became silent as they each scanned the magazines that surrounded them as they waited for their turn with the cashier.

After a few moments, Ethan turned his attention from the magazines and surprisingly made eye contact with an older gentleman who had stepped in line behind them. Ethan uncomfortably glanced away.

"By the looks of your face, it seems that you have gotten yourself into a fight, young man," declared the stranger.

Ethan's dad quickly realized the awkward situation that had just arisen and politely responded to the man, "You *might* describe it that way. That's a birthmark on my son's face. Each day of his life, he battles with the fact that he has something that makes him look different than most people. Some days he encounters circumstances that leave him feeling like he's been beaten up by the neighborhood bully. I constantly remind him that what makes him different can either beat him down or it can make him stronger. Thankfully, my son usually chooses to be stronger. In my opinion, that makes him a hero, wouldn't you agree?"

The older gentleman's face blushed with embarrassment as he stammered, "I am so sorry. I had no idea..."

Ethan's dad kindly interrupted, "No need for apologies. It was an honest mistake. I should thank you because you gave me an opportunity to brag on my son to a complete stranger in the hardware store. I hope you find Ethan's story an encouragement to you. Maybe the next time you feel beaten down by life, you will be reminded of Ethan's story and be motivated to choose to be strong."

In awe, the stranger offered a manly handshake to Ethan and declared, "Ethan, my name is John, and it is very nice to meet you. I hope you accept my apology. Your story is certainly an encouraging one, and I am glad to know it.

Ethan answered, "It's okay," as he bashfully shoved his hands into his pockets.

QUESTIONS TO DISCUSS

➢ How do you think John felt when he realized he was wrong when he assumed that Ethan's birthmark was a result of being hit in the face?

➢ When a person assumes something false about you, how do you typically respond?

THOUGHTS TO CONSIDER

When someone assumes something false about us, it is very easy to become offended and angry, especially if we allow others to define how we see ourselves. Unfortunately, society's opinion of what is cool or good is not always a healthy or accurate view. To make matters even more confusing, society's opinions are constantly changing. What's cool today may be entirely different tomorrow. If we allow society to define how we view ourselves, we set ourselves up for an ever changing roller coaster of emotions. This is unhealthy and not how God wants us to live.

God is the same today as he was yesterday, and He will be the same tomorrow. His love, mercy and grace for you is constant, and it will never end. God wonderfully made you, and you will always be precious to Him. It is important that you regularly study what God says about you, so that you know who you truly are, and so that you will not be moved by how others view you.

PRAYER

Dear heavenly Father,

Thank You for staying the same good God that You have always been. Please help me to remind myself of how You see me. I am grateful that I will always be special to You. In Jesus' name, I pray. Amen.

DAY 3

DAILY CONFESSION

God wonderfully made me, and I am precious[1] to Him.

MEMORY SCRIPTURE

I praise you because I am fearfully and wonderfully made; your works are wonderful, I know that full well. Psalm 139:14

ETHAN'S STORY CONTINUED

"Ethan, it's time for you to clean up your room and hop into bed. We've had a busy day today working on the treehouse, and you need some rest," Ethan's dad stated as he stepped into his bedroom.

"Dad, I've been thinking about what happened at the hardware store today. When John saw my face, he just assumed that my birthmark was from a fight. He probably thought I was a kid who's always in trouble. Why are people so mean?" Ethan asked.

"That's a great question. Sometimes people have so much heartache or anger from their own personal problems, that they just naturally treat others cruelly. Many times, they are so sidetracked by their own feelings, they're unaware of the damage they do to others. In John's case, I don't think that's the explanation. John just had a lack of information. He's probably never known of anyone with a visible birthmark. Most likely, the only time that he has seen a mark similar to yours, it was due to an injury, like from a fight," his dad replied.

"I hadn't thought about that," Ethan admitted.

"It doesn't make rudeness or cruelty right or justified; however, when someone is rude, it helps to think about the other person's viewpoint. It helps us to understand the situation a little bit better," his dad paused as he and Ethan considered that thought. Then, he proceeded, "Ethan, I want you to know it would have been very easy for me to have responded to John in anger. If I had responded that way, you and I might have felt justified for a few moments, but our anger would have lingered, and quite possibly have ruined a great day. Because I chose to speak the truth with grace and mercy, I had the opportunity to remind you of how I see you, and we made a positive impact on John and the others who overheard our conversation. Every conflict you have in life, whether big or small, you have a choice. You can choose to be angry and bitter, or you can choose to make the best of the situation. Sometimes, it's very difficult to make the better choice, but in the end you will benefit from it."

QUESTIONS TO DISCUSS

  ➤ How would Ethan have felt if his dad would have responded to John in anger?

  ➤ What if Ethan's father was wrong about John, and John truly meant to be cruel to Ethan?

THOUGHTS TO CONSIDER

Not much in Ethan's situation changes if Ethan's father was wrong about John, unless Ethan continued to think John was unkind. If he did so and continued to dwell on those negative thoughts, Ethan would probably become angrier toward the situation. That change would only complicate matters. Unfortunately, the fact is, we never truly know what takes place in someone else's mind or heart. And, ultimately, God doesn't want us to judge others. We are only responsible for our actions, regardless of the actions of others.

Even if you make one million bad choices, God's love for you will never stop, and He will always have good plans for you. He always has hope for your future. God wants you to extend His hope to others. He wants you to think the best of others. Be confident that you were wonderfully made by God and that you are precious to Him. When someone doesn't behave as you had hoped, you will know that their behavior doesn't change who you are. You are still wonderfully made and precious to God regardless of what anyone else says or how anyone treats you.

PRAYER

Dear heavenly Father,

Thank You for having hope for me. Please help me to realize ways that I can extend your hope to other people in my life. I am grateful that nothing can change your hope for me. In Jesus' name, I pray. Amen.

DAY 4

DAILY CONFESSION

God wonderfully made me, and I am precious[1] to Him.

MEMORY SCRIPTURE

I praise you because I am fearfully and wonderfully made; your works are wonderful, I know that full well. Psalm 139:14

ETHAN'S STORY CONTINUED

"You can't catch me!" Ethan's younger sister taunted as she sped ahead of him on her bike.

"I'm catching up to you!" he teased back. Sometimes his sister, Harper, drove him nuts, but most of the time he loved being with her. He was proud of how well she was learning to ride her "big girl bike" and had decided he would let her beat him, but not by *too* much.

"I beat you!" Harper triumphantly declared as she halted to a stop at the end of their neighborhood street.

"You're pretty fast on that new bike, Harper. Good job!" Ethan encouraged her as he stopped near her.

As Ethan reached out to give his sister a high five, Nick approached them. Nick lived on the opposite side of the neighborhood, but he had ridden his bike to Ethan's side of the neighborhood a few times. He had only lived in his house for a couple of months, and Ethan didn't know much about him.

"You guys wanna race me back to your house?" Nick challenged.

"Sure," Harper accepted.

Ethan had a sinking feeling in his stomach because he knew there was no way that Harper could keep up with Nick. On Harper's command all three kids sped toward the other end of the street. Nick was the first to arrive at Ethan's house.

"You couldn't even keep up with me!" laughed Nick.

Harper glared at Nick with contempt.

"Aw, come on, don't be a sore loser," chided Nick.

"Don't gloat," Ethan returned.

Nick rolled his eyes. "Hey, what's wrong with your face?" he asked Ethan.

"It's a birthmark. I was born with it," Ethan answered.

"It looks weird. Can't you get rid of it?" replied Nick.

"My brother does *not* look weird. You're just a big bully!" Harper defensively yelled.

"Harper, it's okay," stated Ethan. Turning his attention to Nick, he admitted, "I wish I could get rid of my birthmark, but we haven't found a way. I know my face looks different, but I am still just a normal kid."

"Wanna race again?" Nick grinned.

"Yeah," Ethan replied. *Prepare to eat my dust this time Nick. I'm not letting anyone win this time,* he thought.

QUESTIONS TO DISCUSS

> ➤ Did Ethan use his dad's advice in his conflict with Nick?
>
> ➤ Does Nick's view of Ethan change God's view of Ethan?
>
> ➤ Did Ethan allow Nick's opinion of his face to change how he viewed himself?

THOUGHTS TO CONSIDER

When someone says something hurtful to us, we often want to respond in anger, just as Harper responded. If Ethan had not made the harder choice, the choice to speak truth with grace and mercy, the outcome would have been much different. Ethan made the better choice, which changed an uncomfortable situation into a positive situation.

Like Nick from the neighborhood and John from the store, people can say hurtful things because they don't have all of the facts about the situation. Nick was clearly curious about the different appearance of Ethan's face. Now that Nick has some understanding of why his face is discolored, he just might be on a path to see Ethan in a different or more positive way.

PRAYER

Dear heavenly Father,

Thank You for your mercy and grace. Please help me to learn to show your mercy and grace to others. Thank You for giving me wisdom. In Jesus' name, I pray. Amen.

DAY 5

DAILY CONFESSION

God wonderfully made me, and I am precious[1] to Him.

MEMORY SCRIPTURE

I praise you because I am fearfully and wonderfully made; your works are wonderful, I know that full well. Psalm 139:14

ETHAN'S STORY CONTINUED

"Let's hurry, Harper. I want to play in the treehouse before dinner," Ethan whined.

"I'm folding the towels as fast as I can," Harper complained back. They knew their mom would not budge on requiring them to complete their chores for the day before they could play outside. It was a beautiful spring afternoon, and Ethan and Harper wanted nothing other than to be outdoors, which made their chores even more grueling.

As Harper precisely folded a large bath towel, she declared, "I don't want Nick to play with us in the treehouse today."

"Why not?" Ethan responded.

"He's hateful, and I don't like him. I don't understand why you're nice to him after he was so rude to you the other day," she explained.

"Yeah, I agree he was rude. Part of me wanted to punch him in the nose," Ethan admitted.

"You should have," Harper giggled.

"Dad taught me the other day that when someone is rude, we can choose how we respond. Sometimes it's harder to make the better choice. Punching Nick in the nose was the easy choice. Refusing to be rude was the harder choice, but I think it was the better one. He should have asked me in a nicer way, but he just wanted to know why my face looks the way it does. Maybe after he's been around me for a while, he will be like you and not even notice my birthmark," Ethan hopefully stated.

Unmoved by Ethan's compassion, Harper replied, "You can make the better choice, but I refuse to be friends with Nick."

Ethan chuckled and shook his head. "You're not even giving him a chance. That's exactly how he started off with me. Do you really want to act the way he acted the other day?" Harper looked surprised and hurt, but said nothing. Ethan pressed on, "Give him a chance. If he keeps being rude, we won't hang out with him anymore."

"Fine," Harper caved in.

QUESTIONS TO DISCUSS

 ➤ Do you agree with Ethan's advice?

 ➤ Was Harper acting similar to Nick?

THOUGHTS TO CONSIDER

God wonderfully made everyone. He desires that we recognize this fact about ourselves and others. God always hopes that we will apply His wisdom to our everyday lives. By hoping the best of Nick, Ethan demonstrated an example of how to extend God's mercy and grace.

Harper, on the other hand, had a harder time extending kindness to Nick. Most of us have found ourselves responding with unkindness, or bitterness, similar to Harper. Hebrews 12:15 teaches us that bitterness causes trouble for us. Notice that the scripture doesn't say that bitterness causes trouble for the person that has wronged us. It teaches us that our bitterness causes trouble for *us*. So, we would do well to quickly recognize our bitterness, ask God to forgive us for it, and ask for His help to quickly eliminate unkindness from our hearts.

PRAYER

Dear heavenly Father,

Thank You for always providing hope for me. Please help me to recognize when I have unkindness in my heart and help me to quickly eliminate it from my heart. Please forgive me for any unkindness I have shown to others. Thank You for always forgiving me. In Jesus' name, I pray. Amen.

DAY 6

DAILY CONFESSION

God wonderfully made me, and I am precious[1] to Him.

MEMORY SCRIPTURE

I praise you because I am fearfully and wonderfully made; your works are wonderful, I know that full well. Psalm 139:14

ETHAN'S STORY CONTINUED

"All hands on deck! The pirates are close!" Ethan cried out as he scrambled up the rope ladder to the treehouse. Nick and Harper followed suit.

"I'll be the lookout, Captain Ethan!" offered Nick as he peered through the telescope.

"Harper, you trim the sails, and I'll take the wheel to steer us to safety," demanded Ethan.

"Aye aye, Captain," affirmed Harper, while she tugged diligently on imaginary sails.

"Hey, Scarface, the pirates are trying to board the ship!" mocked Nick.

"My name is *Captain Ethan,*" Ethan corrected him, irritation beginning to rise in his voice.

"Whatever, Scarface!" Nick stated defiantly.

"This is the last time that I am going to ask you to *not* call me Scarface," resisted Ethan.

"I can call you anything I want," Nick objected as he left the telescope and faced Ethan.

"Then you need to find somewhere else to play," Ethan said matter-of-factly.

"You can't make me leave," laughed Nick. Ethan cocked his head to the side and raised an eyebrow. Harper moved closer to her brother.

"Oh, yes, we can. This is *our* house," threatened Harper. Nick paused considering her warning, then shrugged his shoulders.

"I was ready to leave anyway," Nick claimed as he climbed down the rope ladder. Ethan and Harper watched in silence as he left their backyard.

"Now I really don't like Nick. I knew we shouldn't have been kind to him," Harper blurted.

"I don't care what he called me, and you shouldn't either. Do you really want to waste the rest of our day being mad at Nick, or would you rather escape the pirates trying to board our ship?" demanded Ethan.

Harper thought about his point for a moment. Next, she faced her brother, saluted him, and in her best pirate accent, she loudly declared, "Let's defeat some scurvy pirates, Captain Ethan!"

QUESTIONS TO DISCUSS

> ➤ Have you changed your opinion regarding the best choice on how to treat Nick?

> ➤ Would you have handled this situation differently?

THOUGHTS TO CONSIDER

We should commit to making the better choice in all situations regardless of how others act. Just because Nick didn't treat Ethan kindly, it does not mean that Ethan made the wrong choice by extending kindness to Nick. In fact, Ethan once again made the better choice when he extended undeserved hope by giving Nick a chance to be his friend. God's instructions for us are laid out very clearly in the Bible. The instructions in no way indicate that our behavior should change when others mistreat us.

What do we do when we are kind to someone, but they repeatedly mistreat us? It is important to remember that God loves you, and you are precious to Him. He does want you to show others His kindness; though, He would not wish for someone precious to Him to continue to be mistreated. We should do our best to remove ourselves from any harmful situations. In addition, we should be as kind as possible when doing so. In today's example, Ethan demonstrated a great balance of kindness to another person, as well as treating himself as someone precious to God. His response to Nick was firm, but not in anger. He resisted Nick, yet he did not return Nick's rudeness. Ethan made the better choice by keeping bitterness from his heart and not ruining the rest of his day.

PRAYER

Dear heavenly Father,

Thank You for being a God of order and balance. Please help me to find a healthy balance in treating others with your kindness, as well as being kind to myself. Please forgive me for any unkindness I have shown to others or myself. Thank You for always forgiving me. In Jesus' name, I pray. Amen.

DAY 7

DAILY CONFESSION

God wonderfully made me, and I am precious[1] to Him.

MEMORY SCRIPTURE

I praise you because I am fearfully and wonderfully made; your works are wonderful, I know that full well. Psalm 139:14

ETHAN'S STORY CONTINUED

"Missed me!" Ethan shouted as he darted across the gym floor in his P.E. class. Just as he dodged the ball thrown by Sam, a second ball, hurled by Sam's teammate, smacked Ethan in the gut. "Ugh! I'm out!" cried Ethan as he turned and walked toward the sideline. His face didn't show it, but Ethan was grateful for the break since all of the running during the game had left him winded.

When Ethan collapsed down on the bench, Mr. Jenkins blew his whistle and announced that class had ended. All but Ethan hurried to the water fountain or to the door of the gym. In irritation that his rest break had ended, Ethan rolled his eyes and slowly stood. Mr. Jenkins approached Ethan.

"Ethan, you're friends with Dylan, right?" inquired Mr. Jenkins.

Ethan was surprised by the question. Dylan was one of his classmates that wore leg braces due to cerebral palsy. Other than that, Ethan didn't know much about Dylan. "Uh, I guess. I mean, I know who he is, but we've never really hung out," Ethan answered.

"Dylan is a great kid. You would really like his sense of humor. If you got to know him, you might realize that the two of you have some things in common. And, to be quite frank, I think he could use a friend. Have you noticed that he is reluctant to engage with the class?" Mr. Jenkins asked.

"Yeah, I've noticed that he usually hangs out by himself. I've never thought much about it before now, though," Ethan answered.

"Well, if you see an opportunity, please try to befriend him. Maybe your confidence could inspire him to have a bit more courage. You never know, Dylan could become a great friend for you," Mr. Jenkins stated.

"Sure, I can do that," Ethan agreed. Mr. Jenkins gave Ethan a thankful smile.

As Ethan walked to his next class, he thought about his conversation with Mr. Jenkins. Because his teacher described him as confident and trusted him enough to ask him to help Dylan, Ethan felt complimented. It occurred to him that he could truly make a positive difference in someone else's life. Excitement filled his thoughts as he realized: He could be used by God.

QUESTIONS TO DISCUSS

➢ How are Ethan and Dylan different?

➢ What might they have in common?

THOUGHTS TO CONSIDER

Ethan's birthmark is much different than Dylan's leg braces. Still, both of them have something that makes them appear different than others. Dylan might encounter some of the same issues as Ethan. If so, Ethan could encourage Dylan, just as others have encouraged him.

God wonderfully created all people. Everyone has that in common. We also have something else in common: hardships in our lives. Hardships, or struggles in life, affect all people living on earth because we live in a world where sin exists. Some people struggle with very obvious things, like Ethan and Dylan. Others struggle with less obvious things like: sickness, difficulty with schoolwork, problems at home, or fear, for example.

When you look at another person, who might seem very different than you, remember that you have more in common with that person than differences that set you apart from each other. When you realize that the *different* person is wonderfully created by God and is precious to Him, it changes how you see that person. You will begin to see the good things about that person. You will begin to have compassion for God's creation.

PRAYER

Dear heavenly Father,

Thank you for wonderfully creating all people. Please forgive me for any unkindness I have shown to others. Please help me to see people from your perspective, and show me ways that I can make a difference in other people's lives. In Jesus' name, I pray. Amen.

DAY 8

DAILY CONFESSION

God wonderfully made me, and I am precious[1] to Him. I am a child of God, and I am loved by Him.

MEMORY SCRIPTURE

See what great love the Father has lavished on us, that we should be called children of God! And that is what we are! …1 John 3:1

MIA'S STORY

Hot tears streamed down Mia's face as she stood in the school restroom. She dabbed her red eyes and face with a tissue and silently commanded herself to stop crying. *I am stupid just like Sophia said, and I am a big baby because I am crying about it*, she thought. Mia replayed Sophia's hateful words in her mind. Her heart ached with embarrassment as she remembered Sophia announcing, "Mia was so stupid that she couldn't even pass the first math test of the year. Everyone knows the first test is just review and is super easy." She couldn't erase the mental image of two girls giggling in response to Sophia's comment. Mia was mostly mortified by the fact that she had bolted out of the lunchroom and into the restroom.

Suddenly, Mia remembered what her mother had told her on the previous day. Her mom had said that God loved her, and that He always hears prayers. She took a deep breath and whispered, "Please help me, God." She reluctantly stepped out of the restroom stall and splashed her face with cool water at the sink. There was no way she was going to face the lunchroom again even if it meant she would have an empty stomach for the rest of the day. Realizing her afternoon class would start in fifteen minutes, Mia exited the restroom and headed to her classroom. She plopped down in her seat and felt her stomach growl with hunger. Mia noticed that her classmate, Emily, was already seated and eating a packed lunch. Not wanting Emily to notice her swollen eyes from crying, Mia avoided eye contact.

"Hey, I have an extra banana. Do you want it?" asked Emily. Mia cracked a slight smile and thankfully accepted the kind gesture.

QUESTIONS TO DISCUSS

> What helped Mia develop courage to leave the restroom?

> How do you typically react when you are embarrassed?

THOUGHTS TO CONSIDER

It is perfectly normal to feel sad or upset when we are embarrassed or if someone says something hurtful to us.

Oftentimes, these stressful situations play over and over in our mind. It is important to recognize that when we dwell on upsetting situations, it can have a devastatingly negative impact on our life.

When someone does something to make you feel unloved or says something hurtful to you, remind yourself that God loves you. His love is bigger and better than any love that you could possibly imagine.

PRAYER

Dear heavenly Father,

There is no greater love than your love. Thank You that I am your child. Please help me to understand how much You love me and to see examples of your love throughout my day. Your love is more than enough for me. In Jesus' name, I pray. Amen.

DAY 9

DAILY CONFESSION

God wonderfully made me, and I am precious[1] to Him. I am a child of God, and I am loved by Him.

MEMORY SCRIPTURE

See what great love the Father has lavished on us, that we should be called children of God! And that is what we are! ...1 John 3:1

MIA'S STORY CONTINUED

66 "How was school today?" asked Mia's mom. Mia felt hot tears sting her eyes once more as she shared her lunch experience. Mia's mom lovingly wrapped her arms around her daughter and kissed the top of her head.

"Sweetheart, Sophia certainly was not kind to you today, but you can't let her negative actions steal your joy," encouraged her mother.

"Sophia *has* ruined my day, and probably the rest of my school year," replied Mia as she slumped down into a chair at the kitchen table.

Mia's mom didn't respond to her comment, but began preparing a snack for the two of them. When she placed a ham and cheese sandwich on the table, Mia immediately picked it up and took a big bite. Her mom sat down beside her and said, "You know, Mia, we live in an imperfect world with imperfect people, which means everyone will encounter things like sadness or loneliness at some point in their lives. The only perfect person that has ever walked the earth is Jesus. He will always love you and never reject you."

"What made Jesus so special that he was able to be the only perfect person?" Mia asked with a mouthful of food.

"Jesus' father is God," her mother answered.

"How is that possible?" questioned Mia.

"God miraculously caused a woman named Mary to become pregnant with Jesus, even though Mary had never had a relationship with a man. The Bible teaches that Jesus never sinned, which means that he never made any mistakes throughout His entire life. He was also a great teacher of things concerning God even when he was only 12 years old. Everyone was amazed with his knowledge."

Mia interrupted, "I thought a bunch of people killed Jesus because they didn't like what He said."

"That's true, Mia. When Jesus was an adult, some people began to realize that there was something special about Jesus, that He was the Son of God. As that news began to spread, there were many religious teachers that didn't believe that He really was God's son. It made them angry that people were spreading the news to the entire region. So, eventually, the religious leaders arrested Jesus, and they were very cruel to Him."

"I bet that made Jesus and God really mad," Mia stated.

"Jesus still never sinned. He never did anything wrong. Regardless of his innocence, they killed Him."

Mia shook her head in confusion. "That doesn't seem fair. Why didn't God cause another miracle to happen to keep Jesus from being killed?"

"Jesus knew that if He allowed the people to kill Him even though He was innocent, that a greater miracle would happen. He knew that He would be receiving the punishment for the sins or mistakes of all people. Because people are imperfect, we are unable to have a personal relationship with God. But, Jesus' death made it possible for us to have a personal relationship with God. That's how much He loves us."

QUESTIONS TO DISCUSS

➢ Has Sophia ruined the rest of Mia's school year?

➢ Was there anything good that happened to Mia at school?

THOUGHTS TO CONSIDER

Sophia might have ruined Mia's lunch break, but she has not ruined her entire school year; at least as long as Mia doesn't allow her to ruin it. While it is healthy to address stressful situations, it is unhealthy if we dwell on those situations. The Bible teaches us that we should think about anything that is good. Rather than focusing on Sophia's cruelty, Mia should focus on the facts that God gave her courage to exit the restroom and that Emily offered her a snack.

Sometimes we can become so focused on the bad things that are going on in our lives that we totally miss the good things. If you find yourself in a situation in which you truly can't find anything good on which to focus, begin to think about God. He is certainly good, and He has good things planned for your future. He has already done wonderful things for you. He sent His only son, Jesus, to die an innocent death just so that you could have a personal relationship with Him. What's even more amazing is that Jesus willingly endured terrible things so that this could be accomplished. He took all of the blame for any mistake you have ever made and will ever make in the future. Because of Jesus, there is nothing that can separate you from the love of God.

PRAYER

Dear heavenly Father,

There is no greater love than your love. I am so glad that I am your child and that there is nothing that can separate me from your love and acceptance. Thank You for Jesus. In His name, I pray. Amen.

DAY 10

DAILY CONFESSION

God wonderfully made me, and I am precious[1] to Him. I am a child of God, and I am loved by Him.

MEMORY SCRIPTURE

See what great love the Father has lavished on us, that we should be called children of God! And that is what we are! ...1 John 3:1

MIA'S STORY CONTINUED

"**M**om, I can't stop thinking about how Sophia was so hateful to me. Today was one of the most embarrassing days of my life. Everyone in my school is going to think that I am a stupid cry baby."

Her mom finished the last bite of her sandwich, and responded, "Yes, Sophia was very cruel to you today. Each time you think about it, how does it make you feel?"

Mia slunk back in her chair and turned her gaze to the ceiling hoping that tears wouldn't pour out of her eyes. "The more I think about it the worse I feel. Maybe I really am nothing but a stupid cry baby."

"Well, I think you have already figured out that dwelling on the situation is not helping you. Tell me something good that happened to you today," her mom instructed.

Mia blurted out, "Absolutely nothing!"

Her mom reminded her, "Didn't God hear your prayer and give you courage to leave the restroom?" Mia said nothing in response, so her mother continued, "God also gave you the strength to stop crying at school. Then, when you went into your classroom, you found your friend, Emily, who shared a banana with you. You would have been miserable all afternoon if you had not eaten that banana. Mia, you need to focus your thoughts on all of the good things in your life. Don't overlook all of God's blessings.

Mia sighed and reluctantly said, "Okay." She was silent as she thought about her mom's advice and then she began thinking about God and what her mom had said about Jesus. "I know you told me that Jesus died. If he is dead, why do you pray to Him?" Mia inquired.

"After Jesus died, He was buried in a cave, and a large rock was used to seal the entrance. Three days later, two women who were followers of Jesus were surprised to discover that the rock had been rolled away. When they entered the cave, they found an angel instead of Jesus. The angel told them that Jesus had been raised back to life. Later, Jesus appeared to many of His followers and confirmed what the angel had told the two women. Jesus now lives in Heaven with God. He is like a link between us and God. He makes it possible for us to have a personal relationship with God."

"Mom, what does personal relationship mean?"

"I pray to God, and I receive wisdom from Him. He helps me with all areas of my life. I guess you could say that He is the ultimate best friend. And, because I have prayed to Him and I have committed my life to Him, when I die, like Jesus, I will also live forever in Heaven with God."

Mia thought about her mom's answer for a moment and then asked, "How can I have a relationship with God too?"

"Well, you have to believe Jesus is the Son of God, He died and was raised from the dead, and is now alive in Heaven. You have to admit that you have sinned, which means that you are not perfect, and ask God to forgive you. Finally, you need to commit your life to God."

QUESTIONS TO DISCUSS

> What does it mean to commit your life to God?

> Have you ever prayed the prayer Mia's mother described?

THOUGHTS TO CONSIDER

Committing your life to God is the most important decision you can make, and it means several things. One thing it means is that you want God to be a part of your life. Furthermore, it means that you are willing to trust God to help you with everything that concerns you. Finally, it entails you making an effort to learn more about God. If you are like Mia's mom and you would like to commit your life to God, turn to the section of this book titled *Believer's Prayer*. It is a simple process, and it is truly the best decision you could ever make!

PRAYER

Dear heavenly Father,

Thank You for giving people an opportunity to have a relationship with You. Please help me to remember that my prayers to You don't need to be anything fancy or special, and all I need to do is just talk to You. I am so glad I don't have to do anything to earn your love. In Jesus' name, I pray. Amen.

DAY 11

DAILY CONFESSION

God wonderfully made me, and I am precious[1] to Him. I am a child of God, and I am loved by Him.

MEMORY SCRIPTURE

See what great love the Father has lavished on us, that we should be called children of God! And that is what we are! ...1 John 3:1

MIA'S STORY CONTINUED

"Mia, dwelling on Sophia's words will probably cause you to be miserable. But, as soon as those thoughts pop into your mind, I want you to remind yourself of what God thinks about you. You are His child, and He loves you more than you can imagine," Mia's mom encouraged.

"Mom, if God loves me so much, why did He let me fail my math test?" Mia angrily blurted.

"Mia, did you ask God to help you with your math test?" asked her mom. Mia's lack of reply answered the question.

"Mia, God created you to have a relationship with him. There are things that He will do in your life, but there are also things that you need to do in order to receive all of the good things He has in store for you. It's kind of like roller skating."

"What? How does roller skating have anything to do with God?" Mia disbelievingly asked.

"You have roller skates in your closet, right?" asked Mia's mom.

"Yeah, but you're not making any sense, Mom." Mia replied.

"Let's say you are sitting at the kitchen table, and you decide you want to roller skate down the street. Can you close your eyes and poof yourself into the street with roller skates on your feet?"

"Don't be ridiculous, Mom."

"You must take the skates from your closet, put them on your feet, and skate out of the door and into the street. God works in the same way. He doesn't just poof you into a place where all of your problems are eliminated. He needs you to ask Him for his help. Next, you need to do what you know you should do. In regard to your math class, you need to ask God to help you improve in this subject. Now, what do you know that you need to do in order to pass your math tests?"

"I don't know what I need to do," Mia answered.

"Well, do you think you could ask your teacher for suggestions?" her mom replied.

"Probably, but I am not going to ask her in front of Sophia." Mia declared.

"I think that sounds like a good start," her mom stated.

QUESTIONS TO DISCUSS

> ➢ When you have thoughts full of doubt or worry, what do you typically do?

> ➢ What did Mia's mom recommend that she do when she thought of Sophia's hurtful words?

> ➢ Is there anything with which you need God's help?

THOUGHTS TO CONSIDER

Dwelling on our problems usually causes us to feel worried, anxious or fearful. Yet, the Bible teaches that God did not give us a spirit of fear, but of power, love and a sound mind. So what should we do if we truly feel worried, anxious or fearful? Well, Philippians 4:8 teaches us that we should focus our thoughts on good things. That means we should think about how God sees us, how much He loves us, and how He never runs out of good plans for our lives. After you allow His truth to sink into your heart and mind, it is impossible to feel worried, anxious or fearful even if you don't have all the answers to your problem.

When a problem arises, we usually can't see how the problem will be solved. God typically reveals just one step at a time. However, when we trust Him enough to take that one known step, another step is revealed to us. Never give up just because you can't see all of the steps you need to take.   God will never abandon you, but you have to do your part.

PRAYER

Dear heavenly Father,

Thank You for being a problem solver. Please help me to trust You even when I can't see the answer to my problems. Thank You for never leaving me alone with my problems. In Jesus' name, I pray. Amen.

DAY 12

DAILY CONFESSION

God wonderfully made me, and I am precious[1] to Him. I am a child of God, and I am loved by Him.

MEMORY SCRIPTURE

See what great love the Father has lavished on us, that we should be called children of God! And that is what we are! ...1 John 3:1

MIA'S STORY CONTINUED

Mia concentrated her eyes on the classroom clock. It was exactly three minutes before Mia's English class was about to end. She had a firm grip on her English and math books. As soon as the class ended, she planned to make a mad dash to the math class in hopes to speak with her teacher before Sophia entered the room. She thought, *God, I hope you answer the prayer I prayed last night asking you to give me courage to talk to my teacher and help me improve my grade.*

The bell rang. Mia sprang out of her seat and walked as quickly as she could without running. When Mia entered the math class, she was the only person in the room other than her teacher. Mia breathed a sigh of relief.

"Wow! Mia, you made it to class awfully quick!" her teacher announced.

"Well, I was hoping to ask you for suggestions on how I can improve my math grade," Mia nervously asked.

"I am glad you made an effort to talk to me," her teacher responded. As she began writing something on a piece of paper, she spoke, "I would like to offer a couple of suggestions to one of your parents, if you don't mind, Mia. I have written my name and phone number on this piece of paper, and I would like for you to have one of your parents call me," she stated as she handed Mia the note.

"Thank you. I am sure my mom will call you tomorrow," Mia replied.

As Mia walked to her seat, her teacher encouraged, "Mia, it is just the beginning of the school year, and you have more than enough time to significantly improve your math grade. Your attitude and the fact that you are willing to go out of your way to talk to me about it proves to me that you will be successful in this class. So, please do not be discouraged."

Mia faintly smiled at her teacher as she put the note in the pocket of her jeans and sat down at her desk. Her classmates began filling the room. Mia silently thanked God for helping her to have a private conversation with her teacher.

QUESTIONS TO DISCUSS

> ➢ Did God answer Mia's prayer for help? How?

> ➢ Do you think Mia was brave by speaking to her teacher?

THOUGHTS TO CONSIDER

When we ask God to help us with a problem, He doesn't wipe our problem into nonexistence. He does give us wisdom, strength and favor. In Mia's case, God used Mia's mom to encourage her to pray for help, which was wise advice. He provided strength to Mia, so that she could be brave enough to speak to her teacher. Finally, Mia received help from her teacher, which was a result of God's favor.

Mia received strength and favor because she prayed to God and asked for help. Can you imagine how different her day would have been had she not prayed to God? It is important to remember that God loves you, and He desires to have a relationship with you. That relationship begins with a simple prayer from you.

PRAYER

Dear heavenly Father,

Thank You for loving me so much that You want to have a relationship with me. Please give me wisdom, strength and favor with my problems. Thank You for always listening to me when I talk to You. In Jesus name, I pray. Amen.

DAY 13

DAILY CONFESSION

God wonderfully made me, and I am precious[1] to Him. I am a child of God, and I am loved by Him.

MEMORY SCRIPTURE

See what great love the Father has lavished on us, that we should be called children of God! And that is what we are! ...1 John 3:1

MIA'S STORY CONTINUED

"Hey, Mia, would you like to eat lunch with me?" asked Emily as they exited the classroom.

"Sure!" she answered. Mia felt slightly braver as she entered the lunchroom with Emily by her side. They made their way through the cafeteria line and sat down at an empty table.   As they chatted, Mia began to relax and thoughts of math and Sophia were pushed out of her mind.

"Are you going to play basketball again this season?" Mia asked Emily.

"Yeah. Are you?"

"My dad signed me up yesterday. Maybe we will be on the same team," Mia replied.

"How cute, the loser team," Sophia mocked. It seemed as though she had appeared out of nowhere.

Mia felt like she had been sucker punched.

"Just ignore her," Emily quietly stated to Mia. Sophia giggled as she walked away with a group of girls.

"I don't know why she hates me so much," Mia said as she tried her hardest to keep from crying.

"I don't think she hates *you*. She's rude to everyone but her two besties. C'mon, let's get to class. I am curious to see the new art project Mr. Miller has planned for us," Emily said with a smile. Mia smiled back at her friend.

QUESTIONS TO DISCUSS

- ➢ How is Emily helping Mia?

- ➢ Mia is accepting of Emily's friendship, but has she expressed thankfulness to Emily?

- ➢ What are some ways that Mia could offer kindness to Emily? In other words, how could Mia be a receiver and a giver of friendship, rather than just a receiver?

THOUGHTS TO CONSIDER

Friends are a gift from God. He doesn't want us to be isolated. He wants us to enjoy our lives with friends, and He wants us to have experiences that make us smile and laugh every day. Oftentimes, He uses our friends to show us His goodness. If you don't have a friend that helps you to have fun, ask God to bring someone like that into your life. Even better, be that type of friend to someone who is feeling lonely or sad.

There are many ways that you can be a giver of friendship. Here are some examples:

➢ Offer help to someone who is having a bad day,

➢ Hold the door open for someone as they enter or exit a room,

➢ Give a friendly "hello" and smile,

➢ Ask someone how their day has been.

PRAYER

Dear heavenly Father,

Thank You for loving me so much that You want me to have a happy life. Thank You for things that make me smile and laugh. Please help me to bring happiness to people in my life. Thank You for helping me. In Jesus' name, I pray. Amen.

DAY 14

DAILY CONFESSION

God wonderfully made me, and I am precious[1] to Him. I am a child of God, and I am loved by Him.

MEMORY SCRIPTURE

See what great love the Father has lavished on us, that we should be called children of God! And that is what we are! ...1 John 3:1

MIA'S STORY CONTINUED

66 **I** placed a call to your math teacher today. We have arranged for you to meet her in the classroom at 4:00 on Tuesday afternoons. She seems to think that with a little extra time with her, you can bring up your grade fairly quickly," Mia's mom informed her.

"I have to stay at school longer than usual?" Mia complained.

"Mia, it is very kind of your teacher to offer her personal time to you. You should be grateful for her help and not complain," her mom lightly scolded.

Mia hesitantly nodded her head in response and quietly sighed. Extending her school day was in no way appealing to her. Suddenly, she remembered the defeated feeling that had swept over her when she received her last failing math grade. She silently decided that staying late on Tuesdays was not quite as bad as failing math.

"How is the situation with Sophia?" her mom inquired.

"Well, Sophia managed to make fun of me *and Emily* today. Emily has been a good friend to me the last few days, and it makes my problems with Sophia seem not as bad as they seemed a couple of days ago." Mia recounted the story of how Emily invited her to sit with her at lunch, and how Emily encouraged her.

Relieved, her mom responded, "I am happy you had a friend to brighten your day."

"By the way, Mom, may I invite Emily over to our house this weekend?"

"We have several things that will keep us busy this weekend. How about next weekend?" her mom suggested.

"Sure, I will ask her tomorrow," Mia answered.

QUESTIONS TO DISCUSS

> ➢ How does Mia plan to extend friendship to Emily?

> ➢ Do you know of someone to whom you could extend friendship?

THOUGHTS TO CONSIDER

When we encounter challenges in life, it is very easy to feel sorry for ourselves and become discouraged. While it is perfectly normal for us to experience those feelings, God expects us to turn to Him for help. He will never leave us in despair. One of the ways that He rescues us is by giving us favor, which is undeserved good things, like friendship.

It is important to focus on the good things He does for us, rather than overlook them and focus on the problem. As we turn our attention to the good things, and stop dwelling on the problem, we realize that the problem is usually not as bad as we had once thought. Take time to think about some of the things for which you should be thankful in your life.

DAY 15

DAILY CONFESSION

God wonderfully made me, and I am precious[1] to Him. I am a child of God, and I am loved by Him. My birth was not an accident.

MEMORY SCRIPTURE

You are worthy, our Lord and God, to receive glory and honor and power, for you created all things, and by your will they were created and have their being. Revelation 4:11

LEXI'S STORY

Lexi flung herself on her bed and buried her head in her pillow. Her tears were partly due to heartache and partly due to anger. Her mind raced with thoughts. *Why did her dad walk out of her life when she was two years old? How could her own mother abandon her one week after her thirteenth birthday? Sure, her mom knew she was being cared for at her grandmother's home, but still, how could she choose to move to a different city without her only daughter?* Her tears began to soak her pillow.

"Lexi, honey, I know you miss your mom. I miss her too. But, you and I are going to be okay. We can get through this together," her grandmother confidently stated.

"What is wrong with me? Why don't either of my parents want me?" Lexi wept.

"Your parents have made a series of bad choices, and unfortunately, those choices are based on problems they have created for themselves. They are not based on anything you have done. It may not seem like it right now, but I know they love you. There is nothing wrong with you. You are a sweet girl, and they are blessed to have you as a daughter. I am so thankful you are my granddaughter, and my home is your home. You will always have a safe and loving place with me," her grandmother reminded her.

"I love you too, Grandma, and I am grateful I always have you to help me," Lexi said through tears.

QUESTIONS TO DISCUSS

> Have you ever felt unwanted?

> What does today's memory scripture actually mean?

THOUGHTS TO CONSIDER

Today's memory scripture means that God created all people on purpose. He didn't accidently make anyone. When He made you, he didn't make any mistakes, or change His mind about you after you were born. Before you were created in your mother's womb, he designed everything about you on purpose. He planned everything about you, from your physical traits to your personality.

God loves His people more than we can imagine. He loves us so much that He gave us the freedom to choose to obey Him or disobey Him. When people choose to disobey God, it creates an opportunity for bad things to happen. It's important to understand that bad things are a result of sin, which is nothing more than disobedience to God. So, the bad things in our lives are not caused by God. In Lexi's case, her parents had made some wrong choices in life, which have created heartache for Lexi. Oftentimes, when people disobey God, they are not even aware of the hurt caused to other people in their lives.

PRAYER

Dear heavenly Father,

Thank You for creating me on purpose. I am so grateful to know that You will never change your mind about me: You will always want me to have a relationship with You. Please help me to remember this truth. In Jesus' name, I pray. Amen.

DAY 16

DAILY CONFESSION

God wonderfully made me, and I am precious[1] to Him. I am a child of God, and I am loved by Him. My birth was not an accident.

MEMORY SCRIPTURE

You are worthy, our Lord and God, to receive glory and honor and power, for you created all things, and by your will they were created and have their being. Revelation 4:11

LEXI'S STORY CONTINUED

"Lexi, it's time for you to roll out of bed," her grandmother said as she gently shook Lexi's shoulder.

Lexi groggily pulled her covers up to her chin and replied, "But, it's Saturday. Can't I sleep just a little longer?"

"What? It's almost 11:00 o'clock! No, you may not stay in bed any longer. You've had enough rest, and I need your help today."

Lexi sighed and threw the covers back as she sat up in her bed. "Why do you need my help, Grandma?"

"While you were snoozing this morning, I have been busy cooking several days' worth of meals for our neighbor, Rick. I need your help with packaging the food in individual containers and cleaning up the big mess I made."

"Is Rick the man who lives in the house at the end of the road?" Her grandmother nodded yes in response. "Why have you been cooking meals for him?" Lexi asked with a confused look on her face. She knew that Rick was an elderly man, but she had never known her grandmother to cook meals for him.

"Rick fell the other day and broke his leg. He's pretty much bedridden for the next few weeks. Melanie, his daughter, is staying with him to help, and she certainly has her hands full with taking care of him and all of his household chores and errands. The least I can do is make some food for them," she sadly stated.

Lexi smiled at her grandmother as she thought about how thoughtful she was. "You are always helping someone. Are you ever discouraged?"

"That's an interesting question. The simple answer is yes, I do battle discouragement from time to time. But, the funny thing is, as soon as I take notice of someone who could use my help, my discouragement begins to fade. Before I know it, I am so wrapped up in helping someone else to have a better day, and I've completely forgotten about my problem. Now, enough questions. You have 5 minutes to dress yourself and meet me in the kitchen. I need your help!"

"Yes ma'am," Lexi responded as she rolled out of bed.

QUESTIONS TO DISCUSS

> ➢ Do you think it will benefit Lexi if she helps Rick?

> ➢ How does it make you feel when you help someone?

THOUGHTS TO CONSIDER

Sometimes God's ways don't make sense to us at first. One scripture that baffles most of us is Acts 20:35: It is more blessed to give than to receive. We all want things in life, maybe it's a new game, or a new pet, or even to earn a position on a sports team. How can we possibly be more blessed to give something away, when we want something for ourselves? There is no logical explanation, but it is true. Maybe the explanation is that God sees things upside-down from us, or maybe he has an amazing sense of humor. Perhaps it's because he created us to have a relationship with Him and the rest of his people. Maybe His blessings are designed to flow from and through relationships. After all, He created all things on purpose. Our lives, to include each day, have a purpose.

PRAYER

Dear heavenly Father,

You are worthy to receive all glory, honor and power. Please show me how each of my days have a purpose. Thank You for teaching me your ways. In Jesus' name, I pray. Amen.

DAY 17

DAILY CONFESSION

God wonderfully made me, and I am precious[1] to Him. I am a child of God, and I am loved by Him. My birth was not an accident.

MEMORY SCRIPTURE

You are worthy, our Lord and God, to receive glory and honor and power, for you created all things, and by your will they were created and have their being. Revelation 4:11

LEXI'S STORY CONTINUED

"There's enough lasagna here to feed Rick for two weeks!" exclaimed Lexi.

Her grandmother laughed, "Start loading the food in the car. As soon as you are done, we will drive to Rick's house. His daughter, Melanie, is expecting us."

Once Lexi had everything situated in the car, she announced, "The food is in the car. Let's get going. I am looking forward to coming home and relaxing on the couch. My homework has kept me from watching much TV, and I plan to make up for it today."

Her grandmother eyed her disapprovingly, but made no comment. "C'mon, let's get in the car."

Lexi was preoccupied with the radio during the short drive. When they pulled into Rick's driveway, Lexi noticed mounds of leaves from the large oak trees in the front yard.

Just as they stepped up to the porch, Melanie opened the front door and greeted them. "I am so thankful for the food. Taking care of dad is a full-time job. It's nice to have some help," she said with a smile.

"We are very happy to help, aren't we, Lexi?" her grandmother nodded to Lexi.

"Yes, although, I have to admit, Grandma did all of the cooking," she smiled back at Melanie.

As they walked in the house, Lexi was surprised to see Rick laying in a hospital bed in the front room. He appeared to be sleeping. There was a table near him cluttered with medicine bottles and a ledger with some sort of markings.

Melanie noticed her glance and said, "Dad is on so many different types of medicines, from blood pressure regulators, to arthritis medication, to pain killers for the broken leg. I am keeping a log of the times and dosages I give to him to make certain he receives what he needs in order to be well."

As Melanie began to busy herself with putting away the food, Lexi's grandmother asked questions regarding Rick's health. Melanie's face clouded with worry as she shared her concerns of her father's failing health. Lexi felt compassion for Melanie as she became aware of her struggles. Lexi could clearly see that Melanie was tired and overwhelmed with caring for her father.

When there was a pause in the conversation between her grandmother and Melanie, Lexi offered, "Melanie, I noticed there are quite a bit of leaves that need to be raked in the front yard. I have some free time this afternoon, and I would like to take care of that if you don't mind."

Her grandmother's eyes widened with surprise, but quickly welled with proud tears. She immediately blinked them away not wanting to embarrass Lexi. "That's a great idea. I can drop you off on my way to the grocery store. By the way, is there anything I can purchase for you, Melanie, while I am out?"

"The two of you are quite a blessing to Dad and me. Yesterday, I prayed and asked God to help me. I had no idea He would answer my prayer so quickly," Melanie responded with a smile.

QUESTIONS TO DISCUSS

> How did Lexi's attitude change?

> Why was Lexi's grandmother proud of her?

> What kind of impact are Lexi and her grandmother making on Melanie?

THOUGHTS TO CONSIDER

At the beginning of the morning, Lexi was preoccupied with what she wanted to do that day. After seeing first hand Melanie's struggles, Lexi's desire changed. Her compassion for Melanie became stronger than her wish to kick back on the couch and watch TV. When her grandmother realized Lexi's attitude had changed, she was proud of her. Lexi learned for herself exactly what her grandmother had tried to explain to her earlier that day: When you focus on the needs of others, your discouragement begins to fade. The next time you feel discouraged, challenge yourself to look for opportunities to help others.

PRAYER

Dear heavenly Father,

It is exciting to see all of the ways that You bless people. When I am discouraged, please remind me that I will feel better if I help someone else. Thank You for always helping me. In Jesus' name, I pray. Amen.

DAY 18

DAILY CONFESSION

God wonderfully made me, and I am precious[1] to Him. I am a child of God, and I am loved by Him. My birth was not an accident.

MEMORY SCRIPTURE

You are worthy, our Lord and God, to receive glory and honor and power, for you created all things, and by your will they were created and have their being. Revelation 4:11

LEXI'S STORY CONTINUED

Lexi's grandmother pulled in front of Rick's house. "I should be back around 5:00. Let Melanie know if you need anything."

"See you later," Lexi responded as she stepped out of the car.

Just before Lexi shut the door, her grandmother said, "I am so proud of you for setting aside your plans in order to help someone else. You are making a big difference in Melanie's day."

"No problem, Grandma," Lexi replied as she shrugged her shoulders. She tried to hide the fact that she felt pretty good about her decision as well.

Lexi immediately focused on her task of raking leaves. Three of the oak trees in Rick's yard were huge and towered over the house. They were beautiful and sure to provide shade to most of the yard during hot summer months; although, they created enormous piles of dead leaves in the fall. Lexi felt a sense of accomplishment each time she stuffed a bag full of leaves, but that feeling diminished each time when she looked back to the never ending piles of leaves. *What was I thinking when I offered to rake these leaves?* she mentally scolded herself. *I can't do all of this work. I should just give up and walk home.*

As these thoughts swam through her mind, she thought of her mom and dad. Sadness and anger swept over her as she reminded herself of how they had walked out of her life when hardships had come. Next, she thought of her grandmother and of Melanie. She knew both of them were facing difficulties in life, and in spite of that they were continuing with their responsibilities and not giving up on doing what was right. Then she remembered that Melanie had admitted that she had asked God for help. As Lexi worked, she whispered, "God, please help me. I want to be like Grandma and Melanie. I don't want to be a quitter." Renewed energy rose up in her as she started stuffing another bag with leaves.

QUESTIONS TO DISCUSS

> How did Lexi become renewed with energy?

> Do you think God answers your prayers?

THOUGHTS TO CONSIDER

Starting something new is typically exciting, but that excitement can dwindle as you progress into the work. This can be true even of something fun, such as an art project, joining a new basketball team, or maybe something simple like playing a board game. Once the newness becomes familiar and repetitious, the project can seem more like a chore rather than a fun activity. What should we do when we lose interest in a commitment?

Deuteronomy 23:21 teaches us that we sin when we fail to do what we say we will do. God wants us to be finishers, not quitters. He understands that we are not perfect, and He loves us no matter the choices we make. However, we can create unnecessary difficulties in our lives when we don't make the better choice. When we are tempted to neglect our commitments, we should ask God to help us. He always hears us when we speak to Him, and He is constantly waiting for us to invite Him to help us with our problems.

PRAYER

Dear heavenly Father,

You are so good to me. Thank You for always wanting to help me with my problems. Please remind me that I need to be a finisher, rather than a quitter. Thank You for always hearing me when I talk to You. In Jesus' name, I pray. Amen.

DAY 19

DAILY CONFESSION

God wonderfully made me, and I am precious[1] to Him. I am a
child of God, and I am loved by Him. My birth was not an accident.

MEMORY SCRIPTURE

You are worthy, our Lord and God, to receive glory and honor
and power, for you created all things, and by your will they were
created and have their being. Revelation 4:11

LEXI'S STORY CONTINUED

"Wow! Lexi, you've made a ton of progress with the
yard!" Lexi was startled when Melanie spoke. She
had been so focused on her task that she was
unware of Melanie's presence. She suggested, "Why don't you rest
a bit on the porch with me? I brought you some water. You must be
thirsty."

"Yes, I am thirsty. Thanks, Melanie," Lexi replied as she laid
down her rake and joined her on the porch. Sinking into a rocking
chair, she stretched her aching legs and feet. "Grandma should be

here in a few minutes. If you don't mind, I can come tomorrow afternoon and finish with the leaves."

"Oh, yes, your grandmother said she would be here around 5:00," her voice trailing off as though she were deep in thought. After a moment, she resumed, "I'm so thankful for your grandmother. She has been a kind woman to me over the years. She goes out of her way to help my father and me. Most importantly, I certainly appreciate her prayers and her godly wisdom."

"Yes, my grandma is the kindest person I know. I would be very sad without her, and I would be very lonely. My parents haven't been around much," Lexi noted.

"Yes, your grandmother has shared some of your family's struggles with me. I want you to know that I have been praying for you, Lexi, and I will keep doing so. Also, I want to encourage you to keep your eyes opened for God's blessings. They may not always come in ways that you expect."

Puzzled by her comment, Lexi asked, "What do you mean?"

"When I was a young girl, I didn't make friends very easily. There was a period of time that I was very lonely. I desperately wanted to have a friend with which to share my secrets and have sleepovers and all of the other things that girls do with their friends. So, I prayed to God and asked Him to help me. There was a girl named Sally who was in my class. Since she was the most popular girl in my class, I was convinced that she could be the best friend I had always wanted. I asked God to make her want to be my best friend."

"Did she become your friend?" asked Lexi.

"Well, a few days later, another girl named Brittany, started making attempts to be my friend. Since I was convinced Sally should be my best friend, I overlooked Brittany's attempts to befriend me. No matter what I did or said, Sally had no interest in being friends with me. One day, I was heartbroken and I prayed to God and asked Him why He wasn't answering my prayers. All of a sudden, I thought of Brittany. I remembered how a few days earlier, she had asked me to go to the movies with her. Next, I remembered that Brittany had helped me pick up my books in the school hallway when I accidently dropped them. I never heard an audible voice from God, but I knew in my heart that Sally was not the best friend for which I had been praying. Brittany was that friend. I had been overlooking God's answer to my prayers all that time."

QUESTIONS TO DISCUSS

> - Does God sometimes answer prayers by giving you an idea in your mind?

> - Have you ever received an answer to a prayer that was not what you had expected?

THOUGHTS TO CONSIDER

God typically speaks to us through other people and by giving us ideas or thoughts into our minds. This seems contrary to what we would expect because all of our conversations with people are audible. We hear the other person's voice with our ears, and we respond to the person with our voice, which they, in turn, hear with their ears.   It would be so much easier to have faith in God if He spoke to us with a loud voice that boomed from a cloud each time we prayed to Him! Despite that, God's ways are more glorious than our ways.

When we would typically have anger, God has forgiveness. When we would typically have hate, God has love. When we would typically feel confused, God has wisdom. When we would typically loose heart, God has strength. Is it really any surprise that God would communicate to us in a manner different to our typical way to communicate?

PRAYER

Dear heavenly Father,

You are so glorious and more wonderful than I can imagine. Please help me to recognize when You are speaking to me. Please help me with any doubts I might have.   Thank You for helping me. In Jesus' name, I pray. Amen.

DAY 20

DAILY CONFESSION

God wonderfully made me, and I am precious[1] to Him. I am a child of God, and I am loved by Him. My birth was not an accident.

MEMORY SCRIPTURE

You are worthy, our Lord and God, to receive glory and honor and power, for you created all things, and by your will they were created and have their being. Revelation 4:11

LEXI'S STORY CONTINUED

Lexi kept her word by showing up the next afternoon to Rick's house in order to finish her task. She was not enjoying the work; regardless, she was proud of herself for not quitting her task.

"Lexi? I thought that was you!" came a voice from behind her. When Lexi turned around she realized it was Morgan, a girl who lived a few houses down from Rick. It had been a couple of years since she had seen Morgan, and Lexi was shocked to see that Morgan had grown several inches.

"Hey, Morgan! What are you up to today?" greeted Lexi.

"My mom asked me to check on Rick and Melanie. But, I think you're the one that could use some help," Morgan chuckled.

"No kidding! The leaves in Rick's yard seem endless," Lexi replied rolling her eyes.

"I don't have any plans this afternoon. I can help you," Morgan said as she immediately bent down and assisted with holding the bag as Lexi raked in leaves.

"Thank you, Morgan," smiled Lexi.

The two girls made impressive progress together as a team. As they worked the girls quickly fell into a comfortable conversation catching up on school, friends and their shared love of soccer.

"So, how long will you be visiting your grandmother?" inquired Morgan.

Lexi peered down at the leaves she was raking and answered, "Actually, I have moved in with my grandma. More than likely, I will be with her for at least the school year, maybe longer."

"Oh..." Morgan didn't press the subject any further. It was obvious her question had made Lexi uncomfortable. "Well, I am glad you live closer to me now. By the way, several kids from our school that live in the neighborhood come over to my house several times a week. We set up soccer goals for some friendly matches. We could use another player. You wanna join us?"

Lexi smiled. "Sure."

QUESTIONS TO DISCUSS

- ➤ Do you think Lexi was surprised to have a friend help her with her task?

- ➤ Have you ever been pleasantly surprised with unexpected help or friendship?

- ➤ Can you think of any ways that you could surprise someone with help?

THOUGHTS TO CONSIDER

Lexi's heart aches to have a loving mother and father in her life. Unfortunately, her parents are not meeting that need, but her story doesn't end there because God will never leave us nor forsake us. When people do not carry out what He desires, He finds someone else to do the job. God is speaking to Lexi through her grandmother and Melanie. He also sent a friend across her path to add kindness and fun to her life.

Lexi showed up to Rick's house to help him with the task of raking leaves. She did not expect to have a friend show up to help *her.* The New Living Translation of Philippians 4:15-19 teaches us that when we meet the needs of others, God will meet our needs. The beautiful thing about this godly principle is that it may not always arrive in a form that we were expecting. God usually surprises us in unexpected ways. It will serve you well to remember Melanie's advice: Keep your eyes opened for God's blessings.

PRAYER

Dear heavenly Father,

Thank You for never running out of ways to bless me. Please help me to recognize the creative ways You meet my needs. Thank You for never leaving nor forsaking me. In Jesus' name, I pray. Amen.

DAY 21

DAILY CONFESSION

God wonderfully made me, and I am precious[1] to Him. I am a child of God, and I am loved by Him. My birth was not an accident.

MEMORY SCRIPTURE

You are worthy, our Lord and God, to receive glory and honor and power, for you created all things, and by your will they were created and have their being. Revelation 4:11

LEXI'S STORY CONTINUED

L exi skillfully maneuvered the soccer ball in Morgan's backyard. So far, she had successfully kept Morgan from stealing the ball from her. As she neared her teammate, Jenna, Lexi prepared to pass the ball. At that moment, Morgan slid in front of Lexi, stealing the ball with a swift kick. Much to Morgan's dismay, her teammate was not prepared to receive the pass, causing the ball to slam into a nearby large potted plant.

"Oh, no!" exclaimed Lexi as she surveyed the shattered flower pot strewn across the paved walkway that bordered the yard.

Morgan's dad exited the back door of the house and asked, "What's all the commotion out here?"

"Uh, Dad, I'm so sorry, but I broke Mom's flower pot," Morgan replied with much regret in her voice. The rest of the girls stood silently waiting to see how much trouble they had caused for themselves.

"Is anyone hurt?" he inquired.

"No," answered Morgan.

"Okay, I'll grab the broom so you girls can sweep up the mess," he said as he walked toward the garage.

"Wow, your dad didn't even yell at us," noticed Jenna. Morgan nodded as she tried to gather the displaced flowers.

Morgan's dad approached the girls carrying a broom, dust pan, and trash bag. "Girls, when you are playing soccer out here, please play toward the back of the yard, away from the items that could easily be broken," Morgan's dad gently directed them.

"Dad, I am so sorry," Morgan said dejectedly.

"Apology accepted, Kiddo. I know you would never do that on purpose. I am glad no one was hurt." He widened his eyes, smiled and said, "And, I am glad you didn't break a window with your power kick!" The girls laughed and were thankful he had broken the tension. "Girls, why don't you all join us for dinner? Morgan's mom just made more than enough spaghetti for everyone."

"Yum! I *am* super hungry," Jenna answered.

"Me too!" Lexi agreed.

QUESTIONS TO DISCUSS

> ➤ Were the girls surprised with Morgan's dad's response to the broken pot?

> ➤ How do you think God feels when you make a mistake?

> ➤ Do you think God is ever surprised with your behavior?

THOUGHTS TO CONSIDER

God is omniscient, which means that He knows everything there is to know about everything. And, why wouldn't He? He created everything you see: the universe, our planet and everything on the planet to include you. Because of this, He is never surprised with anything you do or will do. He hopes that you will make right choices. When you make a mistake, He immediately forgives you, and He has a plan of rescue just waiting for you. If you have messed up, here is what you should do:

1. Admit to God that you made a mistake, and ask Him for forgiveness.

2. Tell God that you receive His forgiveness and thank Him for it.

3. Ask God to show you what you need to do to overcome any consequences of your mistake.

It's as simple as that! There is never a period of time that God will be mad at you, and there is nothing that you need to do in order to earn His forgiveness, love, mercy or kindness. All of his good qualities are based on who He is, rather than who you are. Even if you made a mistake in every moment of your entire life, God still loves you just the same. He continuously offers His kindness, forgiveness and mercy to you.

PRAYER

Dear heavenly Father,

Thank You for never becoming mad at me. Please help me to remember that I will never have to earn your love or forgiveness. Thank You for teaching me about your goodness. In Jesus' name, I pray. Amen.

DAY 22

DAILY CONFESSION

God wonderfully made me, and I am precious[1] to Him. I am a child of God, and I am loved by Him. My birth was not an accident. I have unique gifts from God that were given to me the moment I was born.

MEMORY SCRIPTURE

We have different gifts, according to the grace given to each of us. Romans 12:6

ALICIA'S STORY

Alicia and her younger brother, Nate, had been working on a puzzle when their mom sat down with a plate of cookies. "Yum!" exclaimed Nate as he shoved half a cookie in his mouth.

"Thanks, Mom. We were needing a snack," smiled Alicia.

"May I help with the puzzle too?" their mom asked.   Nate and Alicia knew their mom loved puzzles just as much as they did.

"Sure," answered Nate. Alicia answered yes by smiling at her mom. All three busied themselves with sorting puzzle pieces and snacking on cookies.

"Alicia, I received a call from Natasha's mom a few minutes ago. They are running a little late, so it might be another hour before she brings Natasha to our house," Alicia's mom stated. Alicia nodded in response but remained silent. "Everything ok, Alicia?"

"Mom, Natasha has been super angry recently. We used to have fun hanging out, but now she spends most of our time saying things that hurt my feelings. I'm not sure what I should do about it," confided Alicia.

"Well, you should be honest with her, but only if you can be full of grace when you tell her. If you start to feel angry or terribly upset, excuse yourself from the room until you can talk to her peacefully. When you're ready, just kindly tell her that you like being friends with her, but what she said hurt your feelings, and ask her to be more thoughtful when she is speaking to you."

Nate chimed in, "God doesn't want us to be angry with people. Sometimes it's hard, but we need to forgive people and try to not fight. God loves you, and He is not happy when people are mean to you. I think you should do what mom said. If that doesn't work, you should find a new friend." Alicia and her mother were surprised at Nate's mature response. After all, he was only 7 years old.

QUESTIONS TO DISCUSS

> ➢ Do you agree with Nate's advice?

> ➢ Have you ever been surprised with wise words from someone younger than you?

THOUGHTS TO CONSIDER

Did you know that God has gifted each person specifically with at least one of these gifts: prophecy, teaching, service, mercy, generosity, leadership, or encouragement? That means that you are also gifted in one of these areas whether or not you have determined which one belongs to you. Today, you learned about the gift of prophecy, and over the next 6 days, you will learn about the other gifts.

Typically, when we think of the gift of prophecy, we think of someone that is able to foretell future events. While foretelling of future events is a prophetic spiritual gift described in the Bible, the gift of prophecy includes other traits as well. The Greek definition of the word prophecy also includes: declaring the purposes of God, whether by reproving and admonishing the wicked, or comforting the afflicted, or revealing things hidden. It is important to remember, true prophets will never teach anything that contradicts the Bible. So, when considering advice from someone, we should always compare it to what the Bible teaches.

Nate has the gift of prophecy. Upon hearing his sister's dilemma, he immediately had an answer. First, he had wisdom regarding the plans and purposes of God, which is that God desires for us to live in peace. Second, he had advice regarding how his sister should treat the problem. Third, he encouraged his sister by reminding her that God loves her, and He has good plans for her. Nothing he said conflicts with information in the Bible.

PRAYER

Dear heavenly Father,

Thank You for graciously giving each person, to include me, unique gifts. Please help me to recognize my gifts and help people in my life to encourage me regarding my unique gifts.   Thank You for helping me. In Jesus' name, I pray. Amen.

DAY 23

DAILY CONFESSION

God wonderfully made me, and I am precious[1] to Him. I am a child of God, and I am loved by Him. My birth was not an accident. I have unique gifts from God that were given to me the moment I was born.

MEMORY SCRIPTURE

We have different gifts, according to the grace given to each of us. Romans 12:6

ALICIA'S STORY CONTINUED

"Ugh! This looks ridiculous. My picture looks more like random blocks of color, rather than a picture that shows perspective," voiced the annoyed Alicia as she sat back in her chair.

"Need some help?" offered her classmate, Ben.

"I'm beyond help. Can you please just do the assignment for me?" she despaired.

"You know I can't do your work for you. That would be cheating. Anyway, you are capable of doing it for yourself. Tell me what you were trying to create."

"Well, I was attempting to draw a Rubik's Cube," she admitted.

"Oh, now I can see what you were doing. It's not bad; we just need to tweak your technique a bit. Here's a clean piece of paper. First, draw the top surface of the cube, with the middle of the cube in the center of the page, as if it were directly in front of you." Ben continued to give Alicia very specific step by step instructions and patiently paused between steps as she carefully completed each task. Even though Alicia had to erase multiple errors and complained each time, Ben remained at ease and patient.

Once the drawing was complete, Alicia admired her work. "Aha! *I did it!* How did you know how to help me?"

"Art is one of my best subjects, and projects that show perspective are some of my favorite pieces of art," Ben humbly answered.

"Well, I usually enjoy art, but this perspective stuff is confusing to me," she confessed.

Ben nodded in agreement, "Most people do find this confusing. Showing perspective is challenging because you are taking a two dimensional surface and attempting to make it appear three dimensional. There are some basic things I can show you to help you understand." Ben began pointing out certain aspects of his perspective drawing. He slowly described the steps he took in order to create his art, allowing Alicia to ask questions as he spoke.

"Oh, now I see what I was doing wrong," realized Alicia.

Mrs. Lansing approached their work table. "Ben, it appears you are once again taking over my class," she teased with a smile. "Your knack of explaining things to the students sure makes my job easier. It is refreshing to have a student with your passion for art. Keep up the good work!"

Next, Mrs. Lansing placed her hand on Alicia's shoulder and waited for Alicia's gaze to meet hers. "Fantastic progress, young lady!"

QUESTIONS TO DISCUSS

> ➤ Ben made a difference in Alicia's day be helping her. Who else benefited from Ben's help?

> ➤ Do you know anyone with a knack for teaching?

THOUGHTS TO CONSIDER

Ben utilized his God given gift of teaching by helping Alicia to understand a tough concept in their art class. He obviously enjoys the subject of art, which makes him passionate about the subject he is teaching. Because of his gift, he is able to explain difficult concepts in an easy to understand manner, which in turn helped Alicia to better understand perspective. Teachers, like Ben, are typically patient with others and easily use multiple methods or tactics to explain an idea. Kinds of methods might include: explaining with words, showing or demonstrating how to do something, or drawing a picture on a piece of paper to explain an idea.

PRAYER

Dear heavenly Father,

Thank You for continuing to teach me about You and how that affects who I am. Please help me to constantly learn more about You and how much I am loved by You. Thank You for helping me. In Jesus' name, I pray. Amen.

DAY 24

DAILY CONFESSION

God wonderfully made me, and I am precious[1] to Him. I am a child of God, and I am loved by Him. My birth was not an accident. I have unique gifts from God that were given to me the moment I was born.

MEMORY SCRIPTURE

We have different gifts, according to the grace given to each of us. Romans 12:6

ALICIA'S STORY CONTINUED

"Alicia! This room is a disaster," exclaimed her mom.

"It's not quite that bad, Mom."

"I have no idea how you found your way to the door this morning without tripping over the clutter filling your entire floor. You may not do anything until this entire room is spic and span," she demanded.

"But, Mom, you said we would see a movie this afternoon," Alicia protested.

"Your sister and I will see a movie, and you will not be going with us if your room isn't clean," her mom answered as she exited the room and went downstairs. Alicia fell back onto her bed with dashed hopes of watching the movie. She felt overwhelmed and could not imagine being able to complete the task.

Her older sister walked into her room. "You need some help?"

"Are you kidding? I need an army of maids! There is no way I can clean my entire room *and* make it to the movie," Alicia complained.

"Don't be overdramatic. You can easily do it with my help." Her sister began piling up the dirty clothes that were strewn across the room. "Pull yourself up and off your bed and start hanging your clean clothes, or I am not going to help you!" threatened her sister.

Alicia eagerly complied with all of her sister's orders over the next hour. Dirty laundry was placed in the laundry room, clean clothes were hung, the furniture was dusted, small items were stowed away in their proper places and the floor was vacuumed.

"Not too shabby if I do say so myself," her sister proudly commented.

Up to that point, Alicia had been so busy with each of the individual tasks, that she hadn't noticed how much progress they had made together as a team. She paused, scanned her room and was surprised to learn that her task was complete. "Wow, my room looks amazing! How did we do that so quickly?" she asked her sister.

"It was easy! Once we got everything organized, there wasn't much left to clean. If you will remember to put things in their proper places when you are finished with them, keeping your room clean won't be that big of a chore," she answered.

"Now you sound like Mom," noted Alicia. "Wait, why have you been so nice to me?" Alicia suddenly realized there would probably be a price to pay to her older sister.

"Hmmm, let's see... How might you repay me?" she teased. "I know, you may do my laundry for me tomorrow," she smugly stated.

"Ugh! Okay, it's a deal," agreed Alicia.

QUESTIONS TO DISCUSS

- ➢ How did Alicia's sister help her?
- ➢ Should Alicia have refused to help her sister with her laundry?
- ➢ Do you know of anyone who is great at serving others?

THOUGHTS TO CONSIDER

God has given some people the gift of service. People with this gift often love to help others with practical everyday tasks, such as: cleaning a room, helping to cook dinner, laundering dirty clothes, or reading to a sibling. The list of tasks is endless. Service minded people constantly pay attention to others and recognize when there might be a need. They are usually quick to offer their help and happy to complete the task at hand.

Alicia's sister has the gift of service, which aided in helping meet the immediate need of cleaning Alicia's room. She could have easily ignored Alicia's problem. She could have easily teased and discouraged her. Instead, her sister recognized the problem, immediately developed a solution, and lead by example with regard to solving the problem.

PRAYER

Dear heavenly Father,

Thank You for blessing certain people with the gift of service. Please help me to recognize this gift in others and remind me to thank them for their service. Thank You for placing these people in my life. In Jesus' name, I pray. Amen.

DAY 25

DAILY CONFESSION

God wonderfully made me, and I am precious[1] to Him. I am a child of God, and I am loved by Him. My birth was not an accident. I have unique gifts from God that were given to me the moment I was born.

MEMORY SCRIPTURE

We have different gifts, according to the grace given to each of us. Romans 12:6

ALICIA'S STORY CONTINUED

"Alicia!" screamed Gracie. Alicia made sure there was no oncoming traffic then dashed across the street to her neighbor's front yard. Tears were streaming down the 5 year old's face as she peered at an injured baby robin.

Panting from her sprint, Alicia asked, "What happened, Gracie?"

Between sobs, Gracie explained, "I was playing outside, and I heard something fall from the tree. I looked around and found this poor baby robin! I saw you in your front yard, so I screamed for you. We have to help him, Alicia. He's hurt, and we can't just leave him here all alone!"

"Okay, just make sure you don't touch him, though. If his parents smell any human scent on him, they will abandon him," warned Alicia. "You stay here and make sure your dog doesn't come near the baby bird. I will find your mom, so she can help us."

After explaining the details to Gracie's mother, both Alicia and Gracie's mom helped assess the severity of the damage to the bird.

"He hasn't moved much, Mom, and I am really worried that he will die if we leave him here. We have to help him!" Gracie pleaded.

Her mom sighed and answered, "Gracie, you would save every injured animal on the planet if I would let you."

"Mom, he's in our front yard. He can't stay here and be safe from our dog," begged Gracie.

Her mom caved in and replied, "You watch over him, and I will make a call to my friend at the local animal rescue. She can tell us what we need to do."

Gracie smiled through tears, "You're the best, Mom."

As her mom reentered the house, Gracie threw her arms around Alicia. "Thank you for helping me save this poor baby bird."

Alicia embraced her sweet hug. "I think you're the one that did all the saving. You have such a big heart. It's one of the things that makes you special."

QUESTIONS TO DISCUSS

> ➤ Have you ever known anyone merciful and kind like Gracie?

> ➤ What kinds of impacts can a merciful person, like Gracie, make?

THOUGHTS TO CONSIDER

People with the gift of mercy have the ability to feel the suffering of another person or animal. When they see that someone has encountered a problem, they are inspired to make things better and often solicit the help of others to create a solution to the problem. They often speak tender and thoughtful words to others. Sometimes they are willing to suffer if they know it will help someone in distress.

Gracie is a good example of someone with the gift of mercy. As soon as she realized the baby bird was injured, she felt great compassion for it. She knew she needed to act on his behalf. Not leaving his side, she demonstrated that she was willing to do whatever was needed in order to help him. She convinced Alicia and her mother to help as well. Grateful for their help, she responded to both of them with tender and kind words.

PRAYER

Dear heavenly Father,

Thank You for creatively giving people specific gifts. Please show me the variety of gifts You have given to people. Thank You for working wonderful things in my life. In Jesus' name, I pray. Amen.

DAY 26

DAILY CONFESSION

God wonderfully made me, and I am precious[1] to Him. I am a child of God, and I am loved by Him. My birth was not an accident. I have unique gifts from God that were given to me the moment I was born.

MEMORY SCRIPTURE

We have different gifts, according to the grace given to each of us. Romans 12:6

ALICIA'S STORY CONTINUED

Alicia watched as her cousin unwrapped her last birthday present. All eyes were intent on discovering if it was the necklace for which they all knew Jacquelyn was hoping. Matter of fact, Jacquelyn and her younger sister, Jessica, both longed for the same necklace. Unfortunately, Jessica's birthday wasn't for another 3 months, and she didn't have enough savings to purchase the piece of jewelry for herself.

Jacquelyn's eyes grew wide as she flipped open the unwrapped box. "Thanks, Mom and Dad!" she exclaimed as she jumped up and gave them both hugs. No one needed to see the contents of the box; they knew it was what she wanted by her reaction. Jessica immediately turned her face away from her sister, embarrassed that she was slightly jealous.

Jacquelyn dislodged the necklace from the gift box and wrapped it around her neck as she walked toward Jessica. "Will you clasp this for me, Jess?"

"Sure," she answered with a forced smile.

Once the clasp was fastened, Jacquelyn turned to face her sister. "Jess, I want you to wear this necklace tomorrow."

"What?" Jessica responded in confusion.

"I'm serious. I know you want this necklace just as much as I do. There is no way that I could enjoy wearing this everyday knowing that you don't have one of your own. I would love to share it with you as often as you would like," said Jacquelyn. Her sister became teary eyed, smiled and hugged her in response.

As everyone began cleaning up the cake plates and cups of punch, Jacquelyn approached her cousin, "Oh, I have something for you, Alicia."

Alicia was startled. "For *me*?"

"Yes, follow me," she declared. As Alicia entered Jacquelyn's bedroom, she noticed a piece of blue clothing and a brown sack on her bed. Jacquelyn picked up the brown sack and handed it to Alicia. "This sack is filled with canned goods. I know you have been working hard to gather items for the local food pantry, and I wanted to help too."

"Oh, thank you!" smiled Alicia.

Next, she picked up the piece of clothing, revealing a soft blue sweater. "I've only worn this a couple of times. When I was trying to determine what pants to wear with it the other day, I remembered that it is your favorite color. I think you will look beautiful in it, and I want you to have it."

"It is my favorite color, and its super soft, but I feel bad accepting a gift from you on *your* birthday," Alicia stated.

"Don't be silly. I want you to have it, and I won't take no for an answer!" Jacquelyn said with a smile.

"Thank you for the food and the sweater. You have to be the most generous person I've ever met."

QUESTIONS TO DISCUSS

➤ How do you think Jacquelyn's generosity affected Jessica?

➤ How does God use generous people?

THOUGHTS TO CONSIDER

People with the gift of generosity often surprise people with their kindness. Like Jacquelyn, they are willing to share everything they possess. They are genuinely unselfish, and they are often found giving things to others. Generous people bring to life Acts 20:35: It is more blessed to give than to receive.

PRAYER

Dear heavenly Father,

Thank You for all the people that possess the gift of generosity. Please continue to reveal to me all of the ways that I am blessed by You. Thank You for hearing my prayers. In Jesus' name, I pray. Amen.

DAY 27

DAILY CONFESSION

God wonderfully made me, and I am precious[1] to Him. I am a child of God, and I am loved by Him. My birth was not an accident. I have unique gifts from God that were given to me the moment I was born.

MEMORY SCRIPTURE

We have different gifts, according to the grace given to each of us. Romans 12:6

ALICIA'S STORY CONTINUED

66 **W**hat are you guys up to today?" Erica asked as she joined the group of kids in Alicia's backyard. Erica lived next door to Alicia, and the two girls spent most summer days together.

Simone, who also lived in the neighborhood, dramatically threw her head back and moaned, "We're dying of heat!"

Erica raised her eyebrows and responded, "You're being a bit of a drama queen. Don't you think?"

Alicia's brother, Nate, came to Simone's defense, "It *is* crazy hot today."

"So, what are you doing about it?" countered Erica.

"What are we doing about the heat? Like we can control the weather, Erica!" Simone rolled her eyes. "Trust me, if I could control the weather, I would lower the temperature by 20 degrees, and I would roll the clouds in front of the sun so we could have some shade."

"Um, Simone, I don't think Erica is suggesting that you control the weather," input Alicia. "So, Erica, you always have some bright idea. What are you thinking?"

"Water is always a good way to beat the heat," answered Erica.

"I've already asked my mom to take us to the pool, but she is too busy," retorted Alicia.

"What about a slip-n-slide? Do you still have one, Simone?" Erica asked.

"No, we wore it out last summer," whined Simone.

Erica thought for a moment then responded, "Well, let's walk over to my house and play in the water sprinklers. Hey, Alicia, do you guys have any water balloons left?"

Before Alicia had a chance to speak, Nate blurted, "Yes, and I know exactly where they are!"

"But, if I play in the water with the clothes I am wearing, I will ruin them! My mother will be so mad," Simone griped.

Starting to become agitated, Erica answered, "Simone, stop whining. Just change your clothes! You can borrow something of mine if you would like."

"I'll grab the balloons, and meet you guys at Erica's house," declared Nate as he headed to the backdoor of the house.

"Okay, Nate." Erica turned to Alicia and instructed, "You change into a swimsuit, and make sure Nate can find the balloons." Alicia nodded in agreement. Next, Erica turned toward Simone, "You go back to your house to change into a swimsuit, then meet me at my house so we can round up some drinks to share with everyone."

"Sure," complied Simone.

"We can always count on you, Erica, to create a great plan! See you in a few minutes," announced Alicia.

QUESTIONS TO DISCUSS

- ➢ How did Erica change the course of the day?
- ➢ Do you know anyone with the same type of take charge personality that Erica possesses?

THOUGHTS TO CONSIDER

Take charge personalities are often characteristic of people that have been gifted with leadership. These people don't normally go along with the crowd. Out of the box thinking is their typical mode of operation as they quickly think of creative solutions to problems they encounter. Others are typically inspired by people gifted with leadership, and they are willing to comply with their suggestions. It is important to note that people with the gift of leadership are *not* harsh people barking orders to others in an attempt to manipulate the situation. Instead, they see the big picture and develop solutions that create a positive outcome for the entire group.

Erica is a great example of a kid with the gift of leadership. Once she became aware of the problematic hot day, she thought of solutions rather than joining the rest of the kids by complaining and failing to develop a plan. She assessed the situation, and she kept thinking of solutions until she found one that won the interest of everyone. Once Erica convinced everyone that her idea would work, everyone was eager to be a part of her plan. Even Simone stopped complaining!

PRAYER

Dear heavenly Father,

Thank You for placing leaders in my life. Please show me how to recognize great leaders. Thank You for the good plans You have for me. In Jesus' name, I pray. Amen.

DAY 28

DAILY CONFESSION

God wonderfully made me, and I am precious[1] to Him. I am a child of God, and I am loved by Him. My birth was not an accident. I have unique gifts from God that were given to me the moment I was born.

MEMORY SCRIPTURE

We have different gifts, according to the grace given to each of us. Romans 12:6

ALICIA'S STORY CONTINUED

Alicia stuffed her sweaty gym clothes in her bag and zipped it closed. As she rose from the locker room bench, her friend, Cammie, slammed her locker shut. With a look of irritation, Cammie flung her gym bag over her shoulder and headed for the door.

"Hey, Cammie, is something wrong?" Alicia asked.

Cammie had been lost in her thoughts and was caught off guard by the question. "Oh, I'm fine." In response to Cammie's answer, Alicia gave Cammie a look of disbelief as she raised her eyebrows.

"Well, I got a bit frustrated during our basketball scrimmage. How did I miss that stupid layup shot? I've practiced it a gazillion times! What is my problem?" Cammie exclaimed as she rolled her eyes in frustration.

"So you missed a layup during a gym class scrimmage. It's not like you caused the team to lose the regional championship. Take a breath and give yourself a break! It's not the end of the world," Alicia comforted.

Cammie just shook her head and sighed in response. "You're right; it's not the end of the world, but, you don't know how much I've been practicing that shot," Cammie said disappointedly.

Alicia put her hand on Cammie's shoulder. "No one.....*no one* is perfect. Maybe your expectations are a bit unrealistic. I'm not saying that you shouldn't keep practicing, but you shouldn't be so hard on yourself when you make a mistake. Even though you missed that last layup shot, you're still the best player in our class, and you have always impressed everyone with you skill. Matter of fact, I remember you smoking us on the court when we first started playing in 3rd grade! That was *before* you started practicing regularly. It's obvious you are naturally talented in basketball. Most of the girls in our class, me included, would give anything to have half of your talent," confessed Alicia.

Cammie's face brightened from her friend's compliment. "Alicia, you always know how to make me feel better with your constant encouragement." She gave her friend a high five and suggested, "C'mon, let's ditch this smelly locker room!"

QUESTIONS TO DISCUSS

➤ How did Alicia impact Cammie's day?

➤ Who in your life is a great encouragement to you?

➤ Can you think of someone who could benefit from some encouragement?

THOUGHTS TO CONSIDER

Alicia's God given gift is encouragement, which simply means to influence or build up someone with words. Encouragers, such as Alicia, often see the best in people, even when others don't. They are fantastic listeners as they seek to accurately understand individual people. Rather than seeing only the actions of others, they try to understand why the person behaved a particular way. Constantly reminding others that they can overcome their fear and failures, they urge them to tackle their dreams.

Romans 12:6-8 teaches us that there are 7 different types of gifts, which are: prophecy, serving, teaching, encouragement, giving, leadership and mercy. Over the last 7 devotionals, you have learned examples of each of these gifts. You may not realize it yet, but God graciously deposited at least one of these gifts into you the moment you were born. If you recognize which gift is yours, make certain you are making use of it. If you don't know what your gift is, don't give up until you figure it out!

PRAYER

Dear heavenly Father,

Thank You for the gift You have graciously given me. Please send people into my life to help me understand which gift is mine and how I may best use it. Thank You for giving me wisdom when I ask for it. In Jesus' name, I pray. Amen.

DAY 29

DAILY CONFESSION

God wonderfully made me, and I am precious[1] to Him. I am a child of God, and I am loved by Him. My birth was not an accident. I have unique gifts from God that were given to me the moment I was born. I am a wise person because God gives me skillful wisdom, knowledge, and understanding.

MEMORY SCRIPTURE

For the Lord gives wisdom; from His mouth come knowledge and understanding. Proverbs 2:6

LOGAN'S STORY

"Well, are you ready for your trip?" inquired Logan's mom.

"Let me check my list." Logan carefully scanned his camping checklist. "I have everything packed, except for my pillow and a flashlight."

"Wow, good job! You packed your items awfully quickly," declared his mom. "You're pretty excited about camping with the guys, aren't you?" she smiled.

Logan nodded in agreement. "Dad said we can roast hot dogs and marshmallows as soon as we set up the tents, and tomorrow Tristan and his dad are going to teach us to fly fish. It's going to be the best weekend ever!"

"I am sure you guys are going to have a great time. Make sure you stay safe by listening to everything your dad tells you, and please be patient with yourself."

Logan wrinkled up his face in confusion. "Be patient with myself?"

"You will be doing many things for the first time this weekend: setting up a tent, sleeping outside, cooking your own food, and fly fishing. Learning something new is certainly exciting, but it can also be challenging. If you are too hard on yourself and become frustrated because something takes longer than you expected, it can easily spoil your day. So, if you start to become frustrated, remind yourself that learning something new takes time and make a point to be patient with yourself. When you need help, be sure to ask God for wisdom. Don't forget: This trip is supposed to be fun." His mom put her arm around his shoulders. "It is certainly going to be quiet around here without my two favorite guys."

QUESTIONS TO DISCUSS

> ➤ How do you think Logan feels about his camping trip?

> ➤ Do you think Logan's mom gave him good advice?

THOUGHTS TO CONSIDER

Why would Logan's mom be concerned about Logan's patience with himself? God hand selected Logan's parents to guide and protect Logan throughout his life. In addition, God gives his parents specific insight into Logan's personality and behavior. This insight or wisdom helps his parents to safeguard him and keep him from danger. When Logan's mom advised him to be patient with himself, she was using godly wisdom to help Logan have a great time during his trip.

Did you know that your parents, whether they are biological, adoptive, or foster, were hand-picked by God to care for you? Your caregivers are not perfect because no person on the planet is perfect, but they have specific abilities and insight that will help you. If that person happens to fail at their job, God will always find another person to assist you. God will never leave you nor forsake you. If you seek His wisdom, He will always provide it to you.

PRAYER

Dear heavenly Father,

Thank You for hand selecting specific adults to help me. Please give my caregivers wisdom concerning me and my needs. Thank You for giving us wisdom when we ask for it. In Jesus' name, I pray. Amen.

DAY 30

DAILY CONFESSION

God wonderfully made me, and I am precious[1] to Him. I am a child of God, and I am loved by Him. My birth was not an accident. I have unique gifts from God that were given to me the moment I was born. I am a wise person because God gives me skillful wisdom, knowledge, and understanding.

MEMORY SCRIPTURE

For the Lord gives wisdom; from His mouth come knowledge and understanding. Proverbs 2:6

LOGAN'S STORY CONTINUED

Logan's dad clipped the last section of the tent to a pole.

"Are we finished with the tent yet?" Logan's stomach was growling, and he couldn't stop thinking of hot dogs and s'mores.

"Now that the tent is assembled, the only thing we have left is to secure the rain fly," his dad answered.

Logan knew the rain fly fit over the top of the tent, and that its purpose was to keep rain from entering the tent. "I don't think there is any rain in the forecast, so we can skip that part, right?"

"You're right in the fact that there are no storms in the forecast. On the other hand, rain showers can quickly pop up. If it starts raining in the middle of the night, do you want to be awakened by a soggy sleeping bag?

Logan sighed. "No."

"It's important to use wisdom when camping. Ignoring wisdom can turn a fun outing into a dangerous situation," noted his dad.

"Have you ever been in a dangerous situation when you were camping?"

"Yes. When I was a teenager, I went camping with some of my friends. Unfortunately, no one remembered to bring a weather alert radio. During the middle of our second night of camping, a thunderstorm rolled into the area. Because we didn't have a radio, we were unaware of the precautions the weather advisors had made earlier in the day. We encountered some pretty strong winds, which destroyed a couple of the tents, including mine. I'll never forget how scared I was when the wind caused part of my tent to cave in on me. One of my friends let me bunk with him, while we waited for the storm to end. That was a really long night, and no one slept much. Needless to say, I learned how important it is to be prepared."

Logan got an uneasy feeling in the pit of his stomach as he imagined having his tent cave in on him. "Uh, dad, I guess you brought a radio?"

"Absolutely!" his dad replied.

QUESTIONS TO DISCUSS

> ➢ How is Logan's dad using wisdom?

> ➢ Is God concerned about Logan enjoying his camping trip?

THOUGHTS TO CONSIDER

Yes! God cares a great deal about Logan's camping trip. As a matter of fact, God cares deeply about all aspects of *your* life. God is crazy about you and thinks about you all of the time. If he had a refrigerator, your life-size picture would be plastered on it! He wants you to have a great relationship with your family and friends. He wants your life to be filled with things you enjoy doing, and most of all, He wants to be a part of every bit of it. If you will seek Him, He will give you wisdom concerning everything, whether it be school, sports, friends, or even camping.

PRAYER

Dear heavenly Father,

Thank You for caring about anything that concerns me. Nothing is too big or too small for You. Please give me wisdom on ways that I can enjoy my life. Thank You for always listening to me. In Jesus' name, I pray. Amen.

DAY 31

DAILY CONFESSION

God wonderfully made me, and I am precious[1] to Him. I am a child of God, and I am loved by Him. My birth was not an accident. I have unique gifts from God that were given to me the moment I was born. I am a wise person because God gives me skillful wisdom, knowledge, and understanding.

MEMORY SCRIPTURE

For the Lord gives wisdom; from His mouth come knowledge and understanding. Proverbs 2:6

LOGAN'S STORY CONTINUED

Logan's mouth watered as he roasted his hot dog over the campfire. Even though a bit of daylight was lingering, Logan was exhausted as he stared at his dinner. He had been so excited about his camping trip that he had a hard time sleeping the night before, and he had worked hard all afternoon and evening helping to set up the campsite.

"Don't become too adjusted to an easy meal like hot dogs. Today you had to cook your food. Tomorrow you will have to catch, clean and cook your food," remarked his dad.

The thought of having to endure even more work dampened Logan's spirits. He pulled his skewer closer to him and decided his hot dog was warm enough to eat.

"Logan, I'm glad you are finally old enough to enjoy camping. Some of my best memories are from the times I have spent camping, and I hope that you enjoy it as much as I do. Being in nature, surrounded by God's creation, reminds me of how awesome our God is. He provides us with everything we could ever need."

"That time when you were camping with your friends, God didn't provide you with a tent that could stand up to the strong winds," Logan argued.

"Let's think about that for a minute. I was well aware of the fact that we needed a weather alert radio though I failed to bring one. Had we received the warnings that were issued earlier in the afternoon, we would have packed up our tents and moved to a safer place. I suffered negative consequences because of my failure to use wisdom, but God in His never ending mercy, made a way for me to seek shelter in a different tent."

"Hmm, I hadn't thought about it in that way," commented Logan.

Noticing that his son was not his talkative self, he thoughtfully watched him as he ate his hot dog. "Today has been a long day, and you've been a big help setting up the campsite. Since Tristan and his dad won't be joining us until tomorrow morning, we can settle in for the night a bit earlier than usual. Both of us could use some rest.

What do you think?"

"I think that sounds great," Logan replied with relief.

QUESTIONS TO DISCUSS

➢ Do you believe that God will provide you everything you will ever need?

➢ When you are lacking something, do you ask God to give you wisdom?

THOUGHTS TO CONSIDER

Do your parents ever seem irritated when you continuously ask them, "Why?" Well, guess what? God never tires of you asking him for wisdom. James 1:5 teaches us that if we lack wisdom, we should ask God to provide it to us. It also teaches us: God will not be disappointed with us for asking, and that He will give us more wisdom than we actually need. We really do have an awesome God!

PRAYER

Dear heavenly Father,

Thank You for never running out of patience or wisdom. Please help me to understand how awesome You truly are. I am so thankful to know that your answer will always be "Yes!" when I ask for wisdom. In Jesus' name, I pray. Amen.

DAY 32

DAILY CONFESSION

God wonderfully made me, and I am precious[1] to Him. I am a child of God, and I am loved by Him. My birth was not an accident. I have unique gifts from God that were given to me the moment I was born. I am a wise person because God gives me skillful wisdom, knowledge, and understanding.

MEMORY SCRIPTURE

For the Lord gives wisdom; from His mouth come knowledge and understanding. Proverbs 2:6

LOGAN'S STORY CONTINUED

Fully rested from the previous day's hard work, Logan had started his morning off with renewed energy and excitement about learning to fly fish. Shortly after his friend, Tristan, and his dad joined them at the campsite, everyone headed toward the river.   Logan and Tristan especially enjoyed spotting birds and squirrels on the short hike to the river. As they stood in the low water of the river, a slight breeze kept the unusually warm fall day at a comfortable temperature. Everything was perfect except for his lack of progress in learning to fly fish. Logan's positive attitude faded with each failed cast of his fishing line. After a loud popping sound, Logan exclaimed in disgust, "What? I can't believe I broke off my fly again!"

"It's really important to pause just a little bit longer between your back cast and your forward cast. Timing is essential," coached Tristan's dad.

Logan tried to hide his frustration. Over and over, he had watched Tristan's dad demonstrate casting the line of his long fishing rod behind him, pause for a short moment, and then cast the line in front of him. Logan desperately wanted to learn to fly fish, and he was truly grateful for the instruction, but he was becoming so agitated that he was having a hard time keeping his mind focused.

"Fly fishing is a difficult skill to learn. You've worked hard this morning. I think we could all use a break," Tristan's dad encouraged.

"I'm thirsty! Let's grab our drinks," Tristan suggested as he headed to the shore.

"I'll rig up your rod, so you can have a break," offered Tristan's dad.

Logan thanked him and followed his friend to the shore. Drinking his cool soda, he thought of his mom and the advice she had given him the previous day. *I could sure use some wisdom,* he thought. Next, he prayed a silent prayer asking God to give him wisdom.

QUESTIONS TO DISCUSS

➢ Have you ever allowed your frustration to spoil a fun day?

➢ Is Logan following his mom's advice?

THOUGHTS TO CONSIDER

At one time or another, everyone has felt frustration like Logan just experienced. Just when everything is going perfectly, something happens to mess everything up. Maybe the frustration was caused by an obstacle like someone saying something hurtful to us, things didn't turn out like we had planned, or we couldn't seem to do something correctly. Whatever our obstacle might have been, it might have quickly spoiled a perfectly fun day. What should we do when we encounter an obstacle and begin to feel frustrated?

First and foremost, we should pray. We should ask God to help us and to give us wisdom regarding our obstacle. He will always give us wisdom. One of the ways in which God provides wisdom to us is through the Bible. Did you know that John 10:10 teaches that Satan desires to destroy good things that happen in your life, but God desires for you to have nothing but good things in your life? God is always on your side!

PRAYER

Dear heavenly Father,

Thank You for always wanting good things for me. Please help me to remember that when I have a problem, I should ask You for wisdom. I am grateful for your goodness. In Jesus' name, I pray. Amen.

DAY 33

DAILY CONFESSION

God wonderfully made me, and I am precious[1] to Him. I am a child of God, and I am loved by Him. My birth was not an accident. I have unique gifts from God that were given to me the moment I was born. I am a wise person because God gives me skillful wisdom, knowledge, and understanding.

MEMORY SCRIPTURE

For the Lord gives wisdom; from His mouth come knowledge and understanding. Proverbs 2:6

LOGAN'S STORY CONTINUED

Logan thought the trout tasted delicious. He felt a sense of accomplishment because he had finally figured out how to cast the fly fishing rod.   In addition, he had stomached through the process of cleaning and filleting the catch of the day. Despite his earlier frustration, he was thoroughly enjoying his first camping trip.

As the guys were finishing their evening meal, Tristan commented, "Logan, you seemed to really get the hang of fly fishing this afternoon."

Logan's dad interjected, "When you were having difficulty earlier in the morning, I thought you might lose interest in fishing. I'm proud of you for not giving up." Then he patted his son on the back. Logan appreciated the compliment.

"I noticed that after we took a break, you seemed less frustrated and more confident. How did you change your attitude so quickly?" asked Tristan's dad. Everyone looked to Logan to hear his answer.

"Before we left on our camping trip, Mom gave me some advice. Since it was my first camping trip and the first time I would try fly fishing, she thought I might become frustrated. She told me to be patient with myself and to ask God for wisdom if I needed help. I don't think I did a very good job of being patient with myself, but when we took a break, I prayed and asked God to give me wisdom," answered Logan.

"That worked?" asked Tristan.

"Well, by the time we got back into the river, I wasn't frustrated anymore, and I trusted God to help me. Each time I tried to cast the line, my mind was focused on everything your dad had coached me to do. So, yeah, I think God answered my prayer," concluded Logan.

QUESTIONS TO DISCUSS

 ➤ Do you think God gave Logan wisdom?

 ➤ Do you need to ask God for wisdom regarding any obstacle in your life?

THOUGHTS TO CONSIDER

God answered Logan's prayer for wisdom. During the break, God helped calm Logan's feelings of frustration, which helped him to think more clearly. When they returned to the river, Logan was able to concentrate on the coaching he had received all morning and apply that wisdom to his actions. Earlier in the day, Logan's impatience turned to frustration, which clouded his mind and took his focus away from the instruction he was receiving. In summary, Logan had been sidetracked.

Satan is very skilled at sidetracking people. He wants to take our focus away from the good things God has done for us by placing obstacles in our way. Oftentimes, obstacles frustrate us to the point that we can't see the whole situation clearly. While it is certainly normal to feel frustration, sadness or anger when we are facing challenges, it is of utmost importance that we remember that dwelling on these emotions will only make matters worse. Like Logan, we should ask God for wisdom to help us to move past those emotions so that we can overcome the challenge.

PRAYER

Dear heavenly Father,

Thank You for knowing all things. Please help me to recognize when emotions are clouding my thinking and help me to overcome those feelings. I am glad that You are the creator of all wisdom and that You are willing to share it with me. In Jesus' name, I pray. Amen.

DAY 34

DAILY CONFESSION

God wonderfully made me, and I am precious[1] to Him. I am a child of God, and I am loved by Him. My birth was not an accident. I have unique gifts from God that were given to me the moment I was born. I am a wise person because God gives me skillful wisdom, knowledge, and understanding.

MEMORY SCRIPTURE

For the Lord gives wisdom; from His mouth come knowledge and understanding. Proverbs 2:6

LOGAN'S STORY CONTINUED

After the guys washed the cooking utensils, themselves, and changed their clothes, Tristan's dad announced, "Boys, you've been a big help today. How would you like to hang out in one of the tents while we clean up out here?"

"Really?" Tristan asked with a relieved tone.

"That would be great! Thank you!" answered Logan. The two boys quickly entered a tent.

"We've already washed the dishes. So, what else is there to clean up?" asked Logan.

"Any little thing we leave out, even a small piece of food or trash can attract animals to our campsite," Tristan replied.

Logan's eyes widened with alarm. "What kind of animals?"

"All kinds...mice, squirrels, raccoons, skunks, even bears. Dad will put all of the food in airtight containers, and then he will place the containers into a cooler. All trash and other items will be stored in special odor proof bags. The cooler and bags will need to be hung pretty high from a tree. It takes a long time to make sure we are safe at night."

"I hadn't thought about the possibility of bears coming to the campsite," worried Logan. "If we are in our tent, and a bear was outside, how would we know it was really a bear?"

"If we are inside the tent, and a bear approached, it might not even make a sound. We would just hear it rummaging through any of our things."

All of a sudden, there was a scratching sound just outside the tent. Both boys froze with alarm. Scratch, scratch, scratch came the sound again. Then there was silence. Scratch, scratch, scratch....then silence.

In a barely audible whisper, Tristan suggested, "Maybe you should pray."

"Boys, everything okay?" Logan's dad asked from outside. The boys relaxed.

"Dad, we heard a weird scratching sound, and we thought it might be an animal," answered Logan.

Logan's dad chuckled. "There are no animals near the campsite. You just heard us cleaning up."

QUESTIONS TO DISCUSS

> Why did Tristan ask Logan to pray?

> Do you pray for wisdom when you are afraid?

THOUGHTS TO CONSIDER

Earlier, Tristan learned that when Logan had a problem, he prayed, and God heard and answered that prayer. So, when Tristan thought they were in danger, his next logical thought was that Logan should pray. God loves it when we share the good things He has done for us with other people. Our testimony, which is when we tell others about the good things God has done for us, is one of the main ways that people learn about God and His love for people. When God answers your prayers, or when you experience His goodness, make sure you tell people about it.

PRAYER

Dear heavenly Father,

Thank You for all of the good things You have done in my life. Please give me opportunities to tell others about the things You have done in my life. I give You all praise and honor. In Jesus' name, I pray. Amen

DAY 35

DAILY CONFESSION

God wonderfully made me, and I am precious[1] to Him. I am a child of God, and I am loved by Him. My birth was not an accident. I have unique gifts from God that were given to me the moment I was born. I am a wise person because God gives me skillful wisdom, knowledge, and understanding.

MEMORY SCRIPTURE

For the Lord gives wisdom; from His mouth come knowledge and understanding. Proverbs 2:6

LOGAN'S STORY CONTINUED

"The weather this morning is perfect for a hike. It's just cool enough to keep us from overheating. Is everyone about ready to start?" asked Tristan's dad.

Logan remained a bit concerned about any animals they might encounter. "Are you sure we won't run into any bears?"

Tristan's dad answered, "Well, I can't promise that we won't see a bear. If we do see one, the most important thing is not to make any sudden movements or noises that might make the bear think that you are a threat. Your risk of being hurt by a bear is much lower than your risk of being hit by lightning. So, odds are, you will not be hurt by a bear. But just in case, in the event that a bear does become aggressive, your dad and I are armed with precautions. There is no need for you to worry. As long as we stay together, we are safe." Logan was comforted by his reassurance.

Tristan, on the other hand, seemed to be deep in thought. Noticing this, his dad said, "Hey Son, don't be worried. We will be careful and stay safe."

"Oh, I am not worried about animals. I was just thinking about how Logan prayed yesterday." Tristan turned to look at Logan, and admitted, "I've been to church, and I know about God, and that Jesus is the Son of God, but I have never prayed to Him. How do I do that?"

Logan answered his friend, "There's really nothing special to it. You just talk to Him like you're talking to me."

Logan's dad agreed with him and added, "Tristan, do you know the story about how Jesus died?"

"Didn't some people tell lies about Jesus, so that He would be killed by the Roman government?" Tristan answered.

Logan's dad replied, "That's exactly right. When He was killed, He was placed in a grave. After three days, God brought Him back to life, and now Jesus is alive in Heaven with God. Do you believe that to be true?"

"Yeah, I do," he answered.

Logan's dad stated, "The most important prayer a person can ever pray is the Believer's Prayer. All you do is admit that you believe that Jesus is the Son of God, and that he died and was raised back to life. Next, you say you want to commit your life to Him."

Tristan's dad added, "He's right. I've prayed that prayer, and I would agree that it is the most important prayer you could pray."

"If you want, I can lead you in the prayer," suggested Logan's dad.

Tristan paused as he thought about it. "Yes, I would like to do that."

QUESTIONS TO DISCUSS

➤ Why is the Believer's Prayer the most important prayer a person could pray?

➤ Have you ever prayed the Believer's Prayer?

THOUGHTS TO CONSIDER

When someone prays the Believer's Prayer, they commit their lives to God. This means that when they die, they will go to Heaven and live forever with God, Jesus and other Christians that have died. A Christian is simply a person that has prayed the Believer's Prayer. The Bible teaches us that anyone who is not a Christian will go to Hell when they die. Hell is not a good place, but Heaven is a wonderful place where there is no sadness, no sickness and no pain.

So, being a Christian and having a promise that you will live for all of eternity in Heaven is a pretty big deal! If you have never prayed the Believer's Prayer, but you want to, read the section in this book titled Believer's Prayer.

PRAYER

Dear heavenly Father,

Thank You for giving me the choice to follow You. Please help me to understand what it means to have a relationship with You. I am grateful that You have created Heaven with me in mind. In Jesus' name, I pray. Amen.

DAY 36

DAILY CONFESSION

God wonderfully made me, and I am precious[1] to Him. I am a child of God, and I am loved by Him. My birth was not an accident. I have unique gifts from God that were given to me the moment I was born. I am a wise person because God gives me skillful wisdom, knowledge, and understanding. I am always saved by God. He always has a plan to rescue me from trouble, even when I make wrong choices.

MEMORY SCRIPTURE

Though I walk in the midst of trouble, you preserve my life. You stretch out your hand against the anger of my foes; with your right hand you save me. Psalm 138:7

MASON'S STORY

Mrs. Walker turned her back to the classroom as she began reading the sentence on the whiteboard. Before she concluded, Mason mimicked the sound of a frog, "Ribbit!" The class erupted in laughter.

Clearly irritated, Mrs. Walker faced the class, which caused the laughter to abruptly stop. It was stone silent as Mrs. Walker eyed each student she suspected might be the culprit. Her gaze rested on Mason, but she said nothing. Becoming uncomfortable with the silent glare, Mason tried to appear innocent and stated, "It wasn't me."

Not breaking her gaze, she responded, "Mason, please go to the whiteboard and read the sentence to the class." Mason slowly rose from his desk and walked toward the front of the room. As he passed the teacher, she handed him a dry erase marker and commented, "You will need this as you label each word with the correct part of speech."

He reluctantly did as she asked. Even though he obeyed her, his attitude was anything but respectful for the rest of the class. Mason was grateful when the class ended. He quickly grabbed his books and tried to avoid eye contact with the teacher as he darted toward the door.

"Not so fast, Mason," Mrs. Walker announced as she signaled for him to come near her. Mason's disrespectful attitude resurfaced as he walked toward her. "You seem to be having a rough time recently. Is there something with which I may help you?" she sincerely asked.

"I'm fine," he answered in a monotone voice.

"Mason, I think you're a great kid, but your recent behavior has been unacceptable. So far, I have been lenient with you, but that is coming to a stop. If you remain disruptive and disrespectful in class, you will be sent to the principal's office. Do you understand?" Mason nodded in response. "Okay, unless you wish to discuss something with me, you may go to your next class." Mason turned and walked out of the room without another word.

QUESTIONS TO DISCUSS

➢ How is Mason being disruptive and disrespectful?

➢ Have you have ever witnessed a student acting as Mason? If so, what did you think about the behavior?

➢ Do you think God wants to help Mason?

THOUGHTS TO CONSIDER

Mrs. Walker's job is to teach the students in her classroom. Mason's disruptive behavior forced her to stop what she was doing and turn her attention to the disruption. Not only did Mason hinder his teacher from doing her job, but he also hindered his classmates and himself from learning. Later, when Mason obeyed his teacher, he continued to cause trouble for himself because of his negative attitude.

As you have previously learned, God has good plans for His people. Do you think God will proceed to have good plans for Mason even though he has made wrong choices? Absolutely! Mason will probably suffer negative consequences because of his wrong choices, but God wants to rescue him from trouble. God is just waiting for Mason to ask him for help.

PRAYER

Dear heavenly Father,

Thank You for always wanting to rescue me. Please help me to remember that You are eagerly waiting for me to ask You for help when I am in trouble. I am thankful for your mercy. In Jesus' name, I pray. Amen.

DAY 37

DAILY CONFESSION

God wonderfully made me, and I am precious[1] to Him. I am a child of God, and I am loved by Him. My birth was not an accident. I have unique gifts from God that were given to me the moment I was born. I am a wise person because God gives me skillful wisdom, knowledge, and understanding. I am always saved by God. He always has a plan to rescue me from trouble, even when I make wrong choices.

MEMORY SCRIPTURE

Though I walk in the midst of trouble, you preserve my life. You stretch out your hand against the anger of my foes; with your right hand you save me. Psalm 138:7

"Y ou really should stop being a jerk to Mrs. Walker," scolded Zoey.

"Whatever! I heard you laugh when my frog started making noise," argued Mason.

"Really? Your frog started making noise? You're acting like a four year-old," Zoey was clearly unimpressed.

Mason didn't have a response, so he started flipping through a book as they both sat at the library table.

"Class, we will leave the library in 5 minutes, so quickly make your final book selections," announced Mrs. Walker.

Mason took a deep breath and was about to make a ribbit sound, when Zoey grabbed him by the wrist and threatened, "Don't even think about it."

Mason jerked away from Zoey's grasp. "What? Are you the library police now? You can't tell me what to do!"

Due to his elevated voice, Mrs. Walker's attention turned to Mason. "Mason, please come with me." Next, she turned to the librarian and directed, "Mrs. Blakely, once the students have made their final selections, please escort the students to our classroom. Mason and I are going to the principal's office."

Mason protested, "But, I haven't done anything!"

"We will discuss it in the principal's office," Mrs. Walker was beginning to lose her patience. Mason shot Zoey a dirty look, but followed Mrs. Walker out of the room. Anger welled up inside Mason with each step he took on their walk down the hallway. *Zoey is going to pay for this,* he thought. As he and Mrs. Walker entered the office, the principal's assistant greeted them and asked them to have a seat as they waited for Mr. Mallory. A sickening feeling crept over Mason as he anticipated what would happen next.

QUESTIONS TO DISCUSS

➢ Do you think Mason deserved to be sent to the principal's office?

➢ What do you think Mason's consequences should be?

➢ Do you think God can save Mason from his trouble?

THOUGHTS TO CONSIDER

Zoey might have been the one to instigate Mason's anger in the library, but it was Mason who caused a scene and attracted Mrs. Walker's attention. Should this excuse Mason from trouble? Not at all. Mason is not accountable for Zoey's behavior; although, he *is* accountable for his behavior. Even though ignoring Zoey's threat would have been the harder choice, it would have been the better choice. Nevertheless, the best choice would have been for Mason to refrain from disrupting his class in the first place.

Typically, when a person makes one bad choice, it makes the next bad choice easier, and the next bad choice easier than the previous one. It can quickly turn into a vicious cycle, which creates one big mess. The earlier a person admits that they are in trouble and asks for help, the easier it is on that person. Ignoring the problem or waiting only makes the trouble greater. In spite of that,

God never gives up hope that His people will call out to Him, even if they have created a massive mess.

PRAYER

Dear heavenly Father,

Thank You for always wanting to rescue me no matter how many wrong choices I make. Please help me to remember that the longer I wait to ask for help, the worse my problem will become. Thank You for never giving up on me. In Jesus' name, I pray. Amen.

DAY 38

DAILY CONFESSION

God wonderfully made me, and I am precious[1] to Him. I am a child of God, and I am loved by Him. My birth was not an accident. I have unique gifts from God that were given to me the moment I was born. I am a wise person because God gives me skillful wisdom, knowledge, and understanding. I am always saved by God. He always has a plan to rescue me from trouble, even when I make wrong choices.

MEMORY SCRIPTURE

Though I walk in the midst of trouble, you preserve my life. You stretch out your hand against the anger of my foes; with your right hand you save me. Psalm 138:7

MASON'S STORY CONTINUED

"Mason, do you agree with Mrs. Walker? Have you truly disrupted her class multiple times?" inquired Mr. Mallory.

Mason felt nervous and outnumbered since both his teacher and his principal stared at him for an answer. "Uh, well, I might have disrupted the class, but I haven't done anything mean or hurtful to anyone. I just do funny things to make the class laugh," Mason defensively stated.

Mr. Mallory was unsympathetic to Mason's excuse. "A funny disruption is still a disruption. Is it true that just yesterday Mrs. Walker warned you that there would be consequences if you caused any further trouble?"

"Yeah, she talked to me yesterday. But, I didn't do anything wrong today. Zoey caused the disruption today," Mason said in frustration.

Mrs. Walker looked at him in disbelief. "Mason, I did not hear a word from Zoey. I heard you speaking very loudly and hatefully to Zoey. If I remember correctly, didn't I hear you say, 'Are you the library police? You can't tell me what to do?' " Mason just shrugged his shoulders and looked at the floor. "It seems to me that you were attempting to cause another disturbance, Zoey tried to stop you, and you became angry with her. Am I wrong?" Mason turned beet red as he fumed with anger, but he said nothing. "Mason, I truly want to help you, especially since you started off the school year so well. Honestly, it's a bit confusing to me. I don't understand why you behaved so well during the first half of the year, and since we came back from our break, you've been acting like a different kid. If you are having some kind of problem, please let us know so that we can help you."

Mason once again turned his gaze to the floor. "I'm fine," he stated with an agitated tone.

Mr. Mallory sighed and stated, "Mason, you will not be allowed to participate in recess for the rest of the week, and unfortunately, we will have to make a call to your parents." Mason let out a deep breath and shrugged his shoulders.

Mrs. Walker stood and announced, "Well, Mason, let's return to class."

QUESTIONS TO DISCUSS

- ➢ Do you think Mason's teacher and principal were trying to help Mason?

- ➢ Was Mason cooperating?

- ➢ What could Mason have done differently?

THOUGHTS TO CONSIDER

By talking to Mason about his behavior and asking him questions, his teacher was trying to find out the reason behind his disruptive behavior. Why would she want to find the true reason for his behavior? Mrs. Walker was trying to find out the actual problem that is causing his negative behavior in order to best help Mason overcome his problem. If Mason had been honest with his teacher and shared his problem, he could have begun his journey to escape from his trouble. Instead, he chose to make his trouble grow.

What happens when we have created a messy problem? How do we begin to turn our mess into a solved problem? The first step is always admitting that we have had a part in creating the mess. We should be truthful to our caregiver about what we have done and share information that might have contributed to the problem. The second step is asking for forgiveness and help to fix the problem. Your caregiver, whether it be a parent, grandparent, teacher, or whomever, has an important job: to help you which includes helping you overcome problems. If you feel that your caregiver is not helping you, ask God to give that person wisdom on how to help you solve your problem. He will hear your prayer!

PRAYER

Dear heavenly Father,

Thank You for being a problem solver. Please give me courage to be honest with my caregivers, and give my caregivers wisdom so that they can help me solve my problems. Thank You for never running out of rescue plans for me. In Jesus' name, I pray. Amen.

DAY 39

DAILY CONFESSION

God wonderfully made me, and I am precious[1] to Him. I am a child of God, and I am loved by Him. My birth was not an accident. I have unique gifts from God that were given to me the moment I was born. I am a wise person because God gives me skillful wisdom, knowledge, and understanding. I am always saved by God. He always has a plan to rescue me from trouble, even when I make wrong choices.

MEMORY SCRIPTURE

Though I walk in the midst of trouble, you preserve my life. You stretch out your hand against the anger of my foes; with your right hand you save me. Psalm 138:7

MASON'S STORY CONTINUED

Mason and his older brother were in the kitchen eating a snack when their mom pulled into the driveway. He worried that his teacher had already called his mom about his meeting with the principal. The two minutes it took for his mom

153

to walk from her car through the front door and into the kitchen felt like an eternity as he anticipated what his mom would say to him. He knew that his mom had enough problems of her own, and he did not want to add more to the list.

"Hi, boys. I am sorry I am home later than usual," she said as she set her things down.

"We were super hungry so we went ahead and grabbed a snack, but we promise to eat our dinner," his brother said between bites. Mason remained silent but studied his mom's face to determine if she had received a call.

His mom looked to his older brother and stated, "Honey, why don't you finish your snack in the other room. I would like to have a chat with Mason." A sense of dread washed over Mason as he bit into his sandwich. As his mom sat down at the table, she addressed Mason, "Your teacher informed me that despite her warnings, you remain a disruption to your class with negative behavior. Is this true?"

"Mrs. Walker is making a big deal out of nothing. Sometimes I just make a funny noise to make the class laugh. It's not like I am being mean to the teacher and not finishing all of my assignments."

"Speaking of work, Mrs. Walker also mentioned that you haven't done very well on your last few assignments, and it might affect your overall grade. Were you aware of this?"

Mason rolled his eyes and leaned back in his chair. "So, I messed up on a few assignments." His mom raised her eyebrows, and Mason raised his voice and answered, "What's the big deal? Everyone makes mistakes!"

"The big deal is your attitude. Mason, you need to work with me not against me. Since your dad moved out of the house, I know

154

it has been tough on you, but it's been tough on me too. I am doing the best I can to figure things out. However, you are making it harder for me to be on your side when you won't even have a conversation with me without a negative attitude." Mason glared at his mom and crossed his arms in defiance. His mom fought back tears. She suggested, "You know, my friend recommended that we try praying. It might be worth a shot, what do you think?" Mason was nonresponsive. "Well, here goes," she said as she bowed her head and closed her eyes.

"Dear God,

Please help Mason and me with his problems at school. Also, please help us to learn how to talk to each other without becoming upset."

QUESTIONS TO DISCUSS

> Why did Mason's mom consider Mason's attitude as negative?

> How do you think Mason's mom felt about their conversation?

> How does it make you feel when someone has a negative attitude toward you?

THOUGHTS TO CONSIDER

One of the first things that typically enters our mind when we think of a negative attitude is harsh or hateful words. Just the same, a negative attitude can also be exhibited by things such as: a sarcastic or unfriendly tone of voice, eye rolling, a hateful glare, or huffing. There is an endless list of behaviors that could be characterized as a negative attitude. When we encounter someone that has a negative attitude, most of us become irritated and frustrated with that person or their behavior. Like Mason's mom stated: It becomes harder to help a person if they act in that manner.

Do you like it when people have a negative attitude toward you? Luke 6:31 states: And as you wish that others would do to you, do so to them. The Bible makes it very clear that if you don't like a particular behavior, then you should not behave in that manner. God's instructions were not created just so that we would have a long list of things we cannot do. God's instructions have been given to us so that we can have a happy life. God intends for you to be surrounded with good things and people that want to help you. When we treat others with kindness, they are much more likely to show us kindness.

PRAYER

Dear heavenly Father,

Thank You for the Bible which is my instruction guide on how to have a happy life. Please help me to know when I am having a negative attitude and give me wisdom on how to change my attitude. Thank You for showing me how to have a happy life. In Jesus' name, I pray. Amen.

DAY 40

DAILY CONFESSION

God wonderfully made me, and I am precious[1] to Him. I am a child of God, and I am loved by Him. My birth was not an accident. I have unique gifts from God that were given to me the moment I was born. I am a wise person because God gives me skillful wisdom, knowledge, and understanding. I am always saved by God. He always has a plan to rescue me from trouble, even when I make wrong choices.

MEMORY SCRIPTURE

Though I walk in the midst of trouble, you preserve my life. You stretch out your hand against the anger of my foes; with your right hand you save me. Psalm 138:7

MASON'S STORY CONTINUED

"Boys, now that we are finished with dinner, you may go outside and play before its time to start our evening routine," Mason's mom announced. His brother bolted to the backyard. Mason lingered in the kitchen and tried to figure out what he should say to his mother. "Mason, what's up?" she asked when she noticed that Mason had not joined his brother.

"Well, I guess...it's just that I don't want to make your life hard, Mom, and well, uh, I'm sorry."

"Well, thank you for the apology, and Honey, *you* don't make my life hard. You and your brother are what makes my life *good*. When you have a negative attitude, your *behavior* makes it difficult for me to help you. Please always remember that whether you have a negative attitude or a positive attitude, or good grades or bad grades, my love for you will not change...no matter the circumstances."

"I love you too, Mom. I don't know why I disrupt my class, but I'm never mean to my teacher."

"Mrs. Walker's job is to teach your class. When you disrupt the class, she is forced to focus on your behavior rather than teaching. It may not seem like a big deal, but several small disruptions can add up to a big chunk of time that Mrs. Walker is not able to do her job. Your disruptions may not be *mean*; but they are certainly disrespectful to your teacher and your classmates. Mrs. Walker has made it very clear that you will be punished if you disrupt the class in the future. Even if you don't see our point of view, you should at least stop disrupting the class, so that you are not punished." Mason did not argue. "I think it would be best if you apologized to Mrs. Walker tomorrow. We had a long conversation earlier today, and I truly believe she cares about you and wants to help you."

"Okay, I will tell her I'm sorry," Mason reluctantly answered.

"Also, I gave Mrs. Walker permission to send you to the counselor's office tomorrow."

Mason whined, "But why? They've already taken away my recess."

"Sending you to the school counselor is not a punishment. She just wants to talk with you. I've heard that she is a very kind lady. It might be helpful, and it's certainly worth a shot. Oh yeah, I also heard that she usually gives snacks to the kids that come to see her. That's a plus, right?" she persuaded.

"Do I have a choice?" asked Mason.

"At this point, no," she answered.

QUESTIONS TO DISCUSS

- ➤ What did Mason do to help his situation in his last conversation with his mom?

- ➤ Why doesn't Mason have a choice regarding a visit to the counselor's office?

- ➤ Does it seem like Mason's mom is trying to help him?

THOUGHTS TO CONSIDER

Apologizing to someone can sometimes be a super hard thing to do. When we have done something for which we need to apologize, we usually have a reason or two that we believe caused us to act that way. For instance, a classmate may have spoken something hurtful to you that caused you to yell hurtful words in return. Or, maybe you were embarrassed by something which prompted you to tell a lie in order to conceal the embarrassment. There is an endless list of possibilities that can lead to bad behavior. Even though we think our actions are justified, the Bible teaches that right is right and wrong is wrong. We are always held responsible for our actions. When we have done something wrong, God wants us to take ownership of our mistake and apologize regardless of the circumstances.

So what should you do if you know you should apologize for something but you don't *feel* like apologizing? You should never let your feelings have complete control of your behavior. When you feel like yelling hurtful things to someone, hopefully you choose different actions because you know that would be wrong. When you feel like staying in bed all day because you don't feel like going to school, hopefully you choose different actions because you know you should attend school. Fortunately, once you make the decision to do the right thing regardless of your feelings, those negative feelings usually begin to shrink. In addition, choosing to do the right thing will save you from negative consequences.

PRAYER

Dear heavenly Father,

Thank You for showing me the difference between right and wrong. Please provide me with strength and courage to do the right thing even when I don't feel like it. Thank You for showing me how to avoid punishment. In Jesus' name, I pray. Amen.

DAY 41

DAILY CONFESSION

God wonderfully made me, and I am precious[1] to Him. I am a child of God, and I am loved by Him. My birth was not an accident. I have unique gifts from God that were given to me the moment I was born. I am a wise person because God gives me skillful wisdom, knowledge, and understanding. I am always saved by God. He always has a plan to rescue me from trouble, even when I make wrong choices.

MEMORY SCRIPTURE

Though I walk in the midst of trouble, you preserve my life. You stretch out your hand against the anger of my foes; with your right hand you save me. Psalm 138:7

MASON'S STORY CONTINUED

"Well, how was your visit with the counselor today?" Mason's mom asked as she prepared the evening meal.

"It was okay, I guess. You were right. She gave me a snack, and that was kind of cool. She asked me a couple of questions, and we just talked about stuff," Mason answered.

His mom stirred the food on the stove and asked, "Will you see her again?"

"Yeah, I think I am supposed to see her every day for the next week."

"That sounds like a good plan. I am happy your visit went well. Did you have a chance to speak with Mrs. Walker?" she inquired.

Mason nodded his head yes. "Before class started, I told her I was sorry. She was pretty nice about it."

His mom motioned for Mason to walk near to the stove and instructed, "Please stir this while I chop the vegetables, and tell me about the rest of your day. How was it?"

"Mrs. Walker divided us into teams to work on our science project. You remember, right? It's the one where we are finding out which foods rot the fastest."

"Oh, yeah. Well, what's the result? Which food rots the fastest?" his mom inquired.

"I think it was the milk," he answered, and then he started laughing.

His mom turned to him with a quizzical expression. "What's so funny?"

As he kept laughing, he answered, "Zoey was on my team, and she accidentally dropped the test tube of milk. When it hit the floor, the smelly milk spilled on Zoey's shoe. It smelled disgusting! Zoey started gagging when she tried to clean it off her shoe. It was awesome!"

His mom sighed and shook her head. "Really, Mason? I bet Zoey didn't think it was awesome."

"She couldn't stop laughing either....between gags. The whole class thought it was hysterical."

"Mason, I am glad you had a good day today. I am also proud of you for doing the right thing by apologizing to Mrs. Walker. That probably wasn't easy for you, but you did it anyway. You made a big step that helped turn your circumstances from bad to good." She smiled at her son as he stirred the food.

QUESTIONS TO DISCUSS

> ➤ How did Mason change his circumstances?

> ➤ Have you ever had a hard time apologizing to someone?

> ➤ What are some ways that your circumstances can change when you apologize to someone?

THOUGHTS TO CONSIDER

James 4:10 states: "Humble yourselves before the Lord, and he will exalt you." How exactly do you humble yourself before the Lord? Well, there are many ways in which you can do this, and one of the ways would be to recognize that God is much bigger than you and admit that you need Him in your life. You can also humble yourself before the Lord with your actions toward people. Here are some examples: apologize when you have mistreated someone, show respect to others by considering their feelings, help someone when they are hurt, and don't remind people of their mistakes. When Mason apologized to his teacher, he humbled himself before God.

The Bible teaches when you humble yourself, God will exalt you. So, what does exalt mean? It means that God will honor you or show you favor. Once you humble yourself, God will cause your circumstances to begin to change from bad to good. He does this by placing people in your life that will help you and encourage you. Anytime you humble yourself, be on the lookout for unexpected kindness and goodness to unfold in your day.

PRAYER

Dear heavenly Father,

Thank You for being a kind God. Please help me to see ways I can humble myself. I believe that You want to surprise me with good things, and I am excited to see what You have planned! In Jesus' name, I pray. Amen.

DAY 42

DAILY CONFESSION

God wonderfully made me, and I am precious[1] to Him. I am a child of God, and I am loved by Him. My birth was not an accident. I have unique gifts from God that were given to me the moment I was born. I am a wise person because God gives me skillful wisdom, knowledge, and understanding. I am always saved by God. He always has a plan to rescue me from trouble, even when I make wrong choices.

MEMORY SCRIPTURE

Though I walk in the midst of trouble, you preserve my life. You stretch out your hand against the anger of my foes; with your right hand you save me. Psalm 138:7

MASON'S STORY CONTINUED

Mason slumped forward on his school desk and rested his chin on his fist. He watched Zoey as she walked to the front of the classroom to take her spot as one of the two team captains. His class was about to play a review game, and each team captain would take turns picking students to be on their team. He felt hopeless as he thought, *Zoey will never pick me to be on her team.*

Mrs. Walker addressed the team leaders, "Captains, you may begin your selections. Zoey, why don't you pick first."

Zoey pursed her lips together as she thought about her first selection, then she announced, "Umm, I pick Mason." Startled, Mason sat up straight and turned his eyes back to Zoey. He wondered, *Did I hear that right?* Zoey just stared back at Mason and then stated, "Uh, Mason, are you going to join my team?"

Mason stuttered, "Uh, well, yeah." He quickly stood up and walked toward Zoey. As the captains proceeded with their selections, Mason's thoughts turned to the time he yelled at Zoey in the library. He knew in his heart that he should apologize to Zoey, but he did not feel like apologizing to her. He thought, *It's too embarrassing to even bring it up. She probably thinks I am an idiot.* Then, he remembered: Just because you don't feel like doing the right thing, it doesn't excuse you from doing the right thing. He silently prayed, *God, please give me the courage to apologize to Zoey.*

A couple of moments later, the team captains were finished with their selections, and Mrs. Walker began giving instructions to the other team. Mason thought, *This is my chance.* His heart pounded in his chest and his face felt hot. He caught Zoey's glance, and quickly blurted, "I'm sorry I yelled at you in the library the other day." He quickly looked away in embarrassment.

"Oh, that's ok. I just assumed you were having a bad day," Zoey replied. Mason breathed a sigh of relief. "Now, let's win this game!" she said as she smiled at him.

QUESTIONS TO DISCUSS

➢ How did Mason humble himself?

➢ Was Zoey merciful to Mason?

➢ When someone apologizes to you, are you typically merciful toward that person?

THOUGHTS TO CONSIDER

Why did Mason know in his heart that he should apologize to Zoey? That inner voice or thought that urged him to do the right thing was God speaking to Mason. Most often that is how God speaks to his people, to include you! So, the next time you have a feeling or thought to do the right thing, obey God's voice and do whatever it is that he is asking you to do.

You might be asking yourself, but how do I know if it is *really* God that is speaking to me? Well, one of the best ways to double check is to ask yourself: Is the action contrary to what the Bible teaches about God? Jesus said that the number one rule is to love God with all of your heart, and the number two rule is that you should love other people like you love yourself. God will never ask you to place yourself or others in danger. So, if whatever it is that you feel prompted to do honors God and shows love to others and yourself, it probably *really* is God speaking to you.

PRAYER

Dear heavenly Father,

Thank You for all of the mercy You have toward me. Please show me when I should be merciful toward others. Thank You for teaching me how to have a good life. In Jesus' name, I pray. Amen.

DAY 43

DAILY CONFESSION

God wonderfully made me, and I am precious[1] to Him. I am a child of God, and I am loved by Him. My birth was not an accident. I have unique gifts from God that were given to me the moment I was born. I am a wise person because God gives me skillful wisdom, knowledge, and understanding. I am always saved by God. He always has a plan to rescue me from trouble, even when I make wrong choices. I am forgiven because Jesus washed away my sin when he died on the cross.

MEMORY SCRIPTURE

In him we have redemption through his blood, the forgiveness of sins, in accordance with the riches of God's grace... Ephesians 1:7

JAYDEN'S STORY

Jayden walked through the large game room of her church. The entire room was buzzing with activity from ping pong matches, to gaga ball, to hopscotch. She smiled at all of the commotion.

"It's wonderful to have a room full of kids, isn't it, Jayden?" asked Mrs. Jones. Jaden's smile grew larger as she nodded her head yes. "The number of kids attending our church has grown significantly over the last year. Our church has begun to make a big impact on the kids of our community, and it is because God has called people like you to volunteer at church. Thank you for all of your hard work. You are evidence that God will even use 12 year old girls to make an impact within the community."

Jayden admired Mrs. Jones, and she was greatly honored by such a kind compliment. "Thank you."

Mrs. Jones spoke again, "As soon as we end the service tonight, I am going to bring a group of workers to the activity room to clean it. Would you mind to stay in the auditorium and make certain all of the power switches are turned off on the handheld microphones? If we leave them on tonight, the batteries will lose power, and they will not work for the Sunday morning church service."

"Sure, that's no problem," Jayden replied.

"Thanks again for all that you do, Jayden," Mrs. Jones commented as she walked toward the door. Jayden was pleased that Mrs. Jones trusted her with important tasks.

QUESTIONS TO DISCUSS

➢ Do you think Jayden likes helping at her church?

➢ Do you believe that God really has important roles for kids like you?

➢ Does God become annoyed with children and wish they would leave Him alone?

THOUGHTS TO CONSIDER

Matthew 19:13-14 describes a time when children were brought to Jesus so that he could pray for them. Jesus' disciples were irritated and attempted to send the children away, but Jesus scolded his disciples for it. Jesus made it clear that he wanted the children to have access to Him. He also made it known that no person should make it hard for the children to come to Him. Another example of how God sees kids is in Matthew 18:10. In this passage, Jesus told the people that they needed to treat children with kindness, because they have their own personal angels in heaven who are in constant communication with God. Whoa! Kids are truly important to God!

You might be thinking: Okay, I understand that God loves kids like me, but that doesn't mean that he has a *purpose* for us. The Bible is full of examples of kids that had a God given job. One example is the famous Daniel who escaped the fiery furnace when he was an adult. Some scholars believe Daniel was only 8-10 years old, when he first stood up for his faith in God. In 2 Kings 5, you can learn about a story in which a young girl gives advice that helps a man to become healed of a serious disease. Additionally, John 6 teaches that Jesus miraculously used a young boy's lunch to feed thousands of people. Surely, the crowd of people were thankful the young boy was willing to unselfishly give away his lunch to Jesus! God uses kids in His plans to bless the world.

PRAYER

Dear heavenly Father,

Thank You for showing me that You love kids and that You have a purpose for kids of all ages. Please help me to understand how much You value me, and show me how I can be your helper. Thank You for my angels that are in direct communication with You. In Jesus' name, I pray. Amen.

DAY 44

DAILY CONFESSION

God wonderfully made me, and I am precious[1] to Him. I am a child of God, and I am loved by Him. My birth was not an accident. I have unique gifts from God that were given to me the moment I was born. I am a wise person because God gives me skillful wisdom, knowledge, and understanding. I am always saved by God. He always has a plan to rescue me from trouble, even when I make wrong choices. I am forgiven because Jesus washed away my sin when he died on the cross.

MEMORY SCRIPTURE

In him we have redemption through his blood, the forgiveness of sins, in accordance with the riches of God's grace... Ephesians 1:7

JAYDEN'S STORY CONTINUED

Jayden hurried into the auditorium of her church. She knew the service would begin in less than three minutes, and she did not want to be late. Each service began with one of her favorite things about church, the praise and worship music. As soon as she found a seat next to her friend, Addison, the music began.

"Hey, I was beginning to wonder if you were going to make it in time," Addison greeted her.

"Me too!" she whispered. Both girls turned their attention to the stage and the music. Jayden leaned close to Addison and whispered, "Did you notice the new singer, Sadie, on stage? This is her first time to sing with the church, and I heard that she is awesome."

Addison scanned the stage trying to find the new singer. "Is that her on the right, in the green shirt?" Jayden answered by nodding yes.

Sadie stepped close to her microphone and appeared to be singing, but the audience heard only the music and no singing. Sadie fumbled with the microphone, but it made no difference. She was clearly embarrassed and nervous. One of the back- up singers stepped up to a different microphone and began singing the song. At the same time, one of the audio workers walked on stage and quickly connected a different microphone to Sadie's microphone stand.

Addison leaned close to Jayden and whispered, "What do you think was wrong with her microphone?" Terror immediately struck through Jayden as she gasped. Shocked by her dramatic reaction, Addison asked, "What's the matter with you?"

Tears began streaming down Jayden's cheeks, as she whispered back to her friend, "It's my fault! I was supposed to turn off the power to the microphones last night, and I forgot to do it before I left the church."

Addison's eyes widened with surprise, but she quickly acted as though it wasn't a big deal and responded, "It's not the end of the world. They already fixed the problem."

Jayden turned her attention back to the stage. Sadie's new microphone was working fine as she belted out the song. Studying Sadie's face and mannerisms, Jayden could tell that the mishap had clearly shaken her confidence on stage, which made Jayden feel like a failure.

QUESTIONS TO DISCUSS

➤ Is Jayden a failure?

➤ How do you feel when you make a big mistake?

➤ What do you think of Addison's response to Jayden's mistake?

THOUGHTS TO CONSIDER

Jayden failed at her task of turning off the power to the microphones, but Jayden is NOT a failure. Jayden is a child of God. Like you, she was made wonderfully by God, and she is precious to Him. He always has a plan to deliver her out of trouble, even when she makes wrong choices. She is forgiven because Jesus washed away her sin when He died on the cross.

Before our world was created, Jesus lived in Heaven with God. When the earth and people were created, God knew that all people were imperfect and would never be capable of living a good enough life to earn His love and acceptance. To solve this problem, God caused Jesus to be born as a human here on earth. He is the *only* human that has lived a completely perfect life. Around the age of 30, Jesus willingly offered himself to be mistreated, punished and killed for all of the wrong things that people had done in the past and would do in the future.

PRAYER

Dear heavenly Father,

Thank You for sending Jesus to wash away my sin. Thank You for redeeming me from all of my mistakes. Please help me to remember that I can be forgiven for anything. Thank You for saving me. In Jesus' name, I pray. Amen.

DAY 45

DAILY CONFESSION

God wonderfully made me, and I am precious[1] to Him. I am a child of God, and I am loved by Him. My birth was not an accident. I have unique gifts from God that were given to me the moment I was born. I am a wise person because God gives me skillful wisdom, knowledge, and understanding. I am always saved by God. He always has a plan to rescue me from trouble, even when I make wrong choices. I am forgiven because Jesus washed away my sin when he died on the cross.

MEMORY SCRIPTURE

In him we have redemption through his blood, the forgiveness of sins, in accordance with the riches of God's grace... Ephesians 1:7

JAYDEN'S STORY CONTINUED

"Mrs. Jones will never *ever* allow me to help with *anything* in the church after what happened today," Jayden commented to Addison at the conclusion of the church service.

Shrugging her shoulders, Addison responded, "So, you forgot about one little thing. It's not like you destroyed the entire church service. I know Mrs. Jones, and she is a very kind person who loves to help everyone. There is no way that she would stop asking you to help at the church."

Jayden wasn't comforted very much by Addison's attempt to encourage her. She shook her head, and stated, "Well, it wouldn't be very smart of Mrs. Jones to trust someone like me to do anything important. Even if she allows me to volunteer, I will not agree to do anything. Today proves that I can't be trusted. I ruined Sadie's first day to sing with the church. I saw her face. She was embarrassed and nervous....all because of me!

Addison felt sorry for her friend as she answered her, "You are being way too hard on yourself. Your one mistake does not begin to compare with the countless great things you do for our church. You are the hardest working kid I have ever known!" She smiled at Jayden trying to cheer her friend. Jayden just shook her head again.

Addison refused to allow her friend to stay in her bad mood, and pressed on, "Our church has a team of volunteers that work together to help each other. When someone makes a mistake, someone else steps in and helps to make things better. That's what teams are supposed to do. Just a few words into the song, one of the backup singers began singing Sadie's part, while the sound technician hooked up a new mic for her. Everything was fixed in less than 60 seconds."

Jayden sighed a deep breath and said, "Yeah, I guess you're right."

Addison smiled and said, "By the way, did you hear the backup singer? She sounded *great*. Maybe that was just the break the backup singer needed to become a lead singer. I bet something fantastic will come from this!"

Jayden chuckled and rolled her eyes at her friend. "I don't know how you can always see the bright side of things," she responded.

QUESTIONS TO DISCUSS

> ➢ Should Jayden quit helping with important tasks at the church?

> ➢ How is Addison helping Jayden?

> ➢ Is Addison's description of a team correct?

THOUGHTS TO CONSIDER

Like Jayden, most people that are in the midst of a dilemma or problem have a hard time seeing all of the facts. Fortunately, Addison helped Jayden to recognize more than her failure. When you experience a problem, ask God to help you see the problem from a different perspective. He just might send an optimist like Addison to help you see the bright side of things!

Anytime you experience a problem, God always wants you to have hope that good things will happen in the days ahead of you. The Bible teaches us this fact: And we know that in all things God works for the good of those who love him, who have been called according to his purpose (Romans 8:28). At the time of your problem, you typically cannot see any evidence of what God is doing behind the scenes to cause something good to happen to you. Despite how it appears, He really is about to cause something good to happen to you. If you truly believe that good things are going to happen in the days ahead of you, your discouragement or sadness will begin to be replaced with joy and peace.

PRAYER

Dear heavenly Father,

Thank You for working behind the scenes in my life to cause good things to happen to me. When I am discouraged or sad, please help me to remember this truth, and help me to remind others that You have good things in store for them too. Thank You for sending Jesus to redeem me from discouragement and sadness. In Jesus' name, I pray. Amen.

DAY 46

DAILY CONFESSION

God wonderfully made me, and I am precious[1] to Him. I am a child of God, and I am loved by Him. My birth was not an accident. I have unique gifts from God that were given to me the moment I was born. I am a wise person because God gives me skillful wisdom, knowledge, and understanding. I am always saved by God. He always has a plan to rescue me from trouble, even when I make wrong choices. I am forgiven because Jesus washed away my sin when he died on the cross.

MEMORY SCRIPTURE

In him we have redemption through his blood, the forgiveness of sins, in accordance with the riches of God's grace... Ephesians 1:7

JAYDEN'S STORY CONTINUED

66 "J ayden!" Mrs. Jones shouted across the church parking lot. Jayden recognized that it was Mrs. Jones calling to her, so she stopped walking, but didn't turn to face her. A feeling of dread kept her from responding to her even though she greatly admired and respected Mrs. Jones. Jayden's mind filled with negativity. *She must know that I forgot to turn of the microphones last night. More than likely, the whole church already knows. No one will ever let me be a part of the team.*

"Jayden!" Mrs. Jones had jogged across the parking lot dodging exiting traffic in order to catch up with her. Out of breath, she huffed, "You left so quickly, I wasn't sure I would be able to catch you."

"I'm so sorry I didn't turn the power off on Sadie's microphone," Jayden blurted as she began to cry.

"Hey! It's not that big of a deal, Jayden," Mrs. Jones stated as she placed her hand on Jayden's shoulder. "You are a super important part of the team. Time after time, you have proven that you are trustworthy, reliable and a hard worker which is exactly why I have entrusted you with so many important tasks."

Jayden ducked her head down in embarrassment and muttered, "Today proves that I am no longer trustworthy, and I am quitting the team of volunteers."

Compassionately, Mrs. Jones responded, "As the team leader, it is my responsibility to check in with my team members to ensure all tasks have been completed with no problems...especially after a big event like we had last night. I failed to follow up with you, which means the problem with the microphones this morning is more my fault than yours." Trying to comfort her, Mrs. Jones placed her arm

183

around Jayden's shoulders and spoke, "Just like every other human that has ever lived, I am not perfect, and no matter how hard I try, I will never be perfect."

Jayden sniffled and commented, "You seem pretty perfect to me."

Laughing, Mrs. Jones responded, "I am *not* perfect. But guess what? God knows I am not perfect, and He loves me anyway. He even knows that I will never be perfect, and He continues to have good plans for me. He will always trust me with important jobs regardless of my imperfections. If God calls me to do a task even though He knows I will not be perfect, I will trust His judgement. When I mess up, it is a great reminder of how much I need God to be a part of my life."

Jayden began to feel better because of Mrs. Jones's honest and encouraging words. "Well, I definitely need Jesus' redemption!" she chuckled.

Mrs. Jones smiled and nodded her head as she said, "We all need the saving grace of Jesus."

QUESTIONS TO DISCUSS

> ➢ Were the negative thoughts Jayden had about herself correct?

> ➢ What kinds of thoughts do you typically think about yourself?

> ➢ What kinds of thoughts do you think about yourself when you make mistakes?

THOUGHTS TO CONSIDER

The negative thoughts Jayden had about herself were not true. The whole church did not know about her mistake, and even if they were aware of it, they would not kick her off the team of volunteers. Jayden has something in common with every other person on the planet: We ALL make mistakes. Thankfully, Mrs. Jones reminded Jayden that everyone needs redemption. Everyone needs Jesus and the truth of God's Word.

When you have unkind thoughts about yourself, you might as well be saying to God, "I don't believe the Bible is true. I don't believe I was wonderfully made and that I am precious to you." Challenge yourself to believe what God believes about you. God is the creator of the universe and everything within it. He has all knowledge and wisdom. He is more trustworthy than anyone you will ever know.

PRAYER

Dear heavenly Father,

Thank You for believing good things about me. When I think negative things about myself, please remind me that You don't want me to think that way. Please help me to remember how You see me. Thank You for sending Jesus to redeem me from my mistakes. In Jesus' name, I pray. Amen.

DAY 47

DAILY CONFESSION

God wonderfully made me, and I am precious[1] to Him. I am a child of God, and I am loved by Him. My birth was not an accident. I have unique gifts from God that were given to me the moment I was born. I am a wise person because God gives me skillful wisdom, knowledge, and understanding. I am always saved by God. He always has a plan to rescue me from trouble, even when I make wrong choices. I am forgiven because Jesus washed away my sin when he died on the cross.

MEMORY SCRIPTURE

In him we have redemption through his blood, the forgiveness of sins, in accordance with the riches of God's grace... Ephesians 1:7

JAYDEN'S STORY CONTINUED

Jayden stepped onto the back patio of her home, and her dog, Sunny, ran to greet her. Jayden plopped down on the ground and petted Sunny as he laid his head on her leg.

Noticing Jayden, her mom stopped her gardening work and thoughtfully approached her daughter. "Honey, how are you doing today?"

Jayden's gaze never left Sunny as she answered, "I'm okay."

Not convinced that she was truly okay, her mother commented, "You seem kind of sad today. Has something happened to upset you?"

Jayden fought back tears as she described her failure to her mom.

"I am so sorry that happened, Jayden." She removed her dirty gloves and sat down on the ground with her daughter. "It sounds like Mrs. Jones has forgiven you. Is that correct?"

"Yeah," Jayden answered as she wiped a tear off her cheek.

"Now it's time for you to ask God to help you forgive yourself," her mom commented.

Jayden looked at her mom with a confused expression, "Why do I need to do that? ...especially when I don't deserve it?"

"God's forgiveness, love or redemption has nothing to do with what we deserve. Matter of fact, there is no way that you can be good enough to deserve anything good from God. He freely gives us all of those things because of who He is, not because of who we are or what we have done. He loves, forgives, and redeems us because of *His* grace."

"Mom, I hear the word grace all of the time in church. It confuses me because I thought grace described the way ballerinas dance, like how they are so elegant when they glide across the stage." Jayden scrunched up her face in a puzzled expression, "Does that mean that God loves stuff like ballet and classical music?"

Her mom answered, "My guess is that God probably likes classical music and ballet just as he likes other styles of music and sports. You are partly right about the meaning of grace, but it has a second meaning too. It's like how the word bat means an animal that flies at night, and bat can also refer to what a baseball player uses to hit a ball." After Jayden nodded that she understood, her mom explained, "The second meaning of the word grace is undeserved goodness from God. He always loves us, always forgives us, and always redeems us even though He knows there is no way we will ever deserve it."

"It's hard to believe that God is able to be that kind," Jayden admitted.

Smiling, her mom responded, "Well, thankfully, He *is* that kind. Would you like for me to lead you in a prayer to ask for God's help?"

"Yes," Jayden answered.

QUESTIONS TO DISCUSS

> ➤ Have you ever received something you didn't think you deserved? If so, how did that make you feel?

> ➤ Do you believe God has grace for you?

> ➤ Why did Jayden's mom think that Jayden needs to forgive herself?

THOUGHTS TO CONSIDER

When you make a mistake, the first step to getting out of trouble is admitting you made a mistake and asking God to forgive you. The very moment you do this God forgives you, and He erases the mistake from His memory. Many times, people make the error of dwelling on their mistake and failing to forgive themselves. In reference to Jayden's case, if she repeatedly dwells on her mistake and fails to forgive herself, she will fail to have joy and peace in her heart, and she will miss out on the good plans that God has for her. She will miss out on all of the grace that God has already freely given to her.

Ephesians 2:8-9 reads: For it is by grace you have been saved, through faith – and this is not from yourselves, it is the gift of God – not by works, so that no one can boast. This scripture makes it clear that when God saves us, he saves us because of His grace. It also specifically states that it is His free gift to us, and there is nothing that we could possibly do to earn it. God designed it this way, so that there is no way that we can brag to another person claiming that we earned His grace.

PRAYER

Dear heavenly Father,

Thank You for giving me the free gift of grace. Because of your grace, I know You will always love me, forgive me and redeem me. Please help me to remember that your grace is the best gift I could ever receive. I am thankful I don't have to work for or earn your grace. In Jesus' name, I pray. Amen.

DAY 48

DAILY CONFESSION

God wonderfully made me, and I am precious[1] to Him. I am a child of God, and I am loved by Him. My birth was not an accident. I have unique gifts from God that were given to me the moment I was born. I am a wise person because God gives me skillful wisdom, knowledge, and understanding. I am always saved by God. He always has a plan to rescue me from trouble, even when I make wrong choices. I am forgiven because Jesus washed away my sin when he died on the cross.

MEMORY SCRIPTURE

In him we have redemption through his blood, the forgiveness of sins, in accordance with the riches of God's grace... Ephesians 1:7

JAYDEN'S STORY CONTINUED

Nervously, Jayden quietly tapped her fingers on the side of her chair. She tried to pay attention to Mrs. Jones as she assigned tasks to the room full of volunteers for the next kids' game night. Scanning the room of volunteers, she realized that she was the youngest person in the room. She thought, *I am crazy for coming to this meeting. I'm too young to be used by God. My last failure proved that I am not trustworthy. Why did I let my parents convince me to come to this meeting?*

"Jayden, about 30 minutes prior to the start of the games, would you mind to draw 3 hopscotch patterns on the ground?" asked Mrs. Jones. "We plan to have a hopscotch tournament for the 5 and 6 year old kids."

"Uh, okay," Jayden stammered. She knew she needed to concentrate on the information Mrs. Jones was discussing, but she couldn't keep her mind from wandering. Negative thoughts filled her mind and distracted her from the rest of the meeting until suddenly she felt someone nudging her chair.

"Earth to Jayden! Hey, the meeting is over, and we are free to leave," announced Cameron, a fellow volunteer as he headed for the door.

"Oh, I was deep in thought. Thanks!" she admitted.

Mrs. Jones approached her and asked, "You seemed distracted today. What's going on?"

Jayden wasn't sure she wanted to talk about all of the thoughts filling her mind. Trying to decide what to say, she fidgeted and answered, "Umm, well, I'm just tired, and I think that is making it hard for me to concentrate."

Not convinced that was the whole truth, Mrs. Jones stepped directly in front of Jayden, forcing her to make eye contact with her and replied, "C'mon, be honest. Tell me what's going on in that smart brain of yours."

Jayden caved in and admitted, "I prayed and asked God to help me forgive myself. Even though I know I am forgiven, I can't stop thinking that I am a failure. I keep having these thoughts that I shouldn't be trusted because I will always make a mess of things. I'm just a kid who makes a bunch of mistakes. It would be ridiculous for God to want me to work in the church."

Mrs. Jones answered, "It's true that you have made mistakes in the past, and it is true that you will make mistakes in the future, but that doesn't mean that you shouldn't be trusted or that you shouldn't work in the church. God loves to give His imperfect people big jobs, so that when those people succeed, it's obvious that God was at work."

Jayden admitted, "But I can't seem to stop my negative thoughts, and once they start that's all I think about."

"When those negative thoughts enter your mind, I want you to replace those thoughts with what God believes about you. You are in charge of your mind. You determine what stays in your mind and what leaves your mind," Mrs. Jones stated.

QUESTIONS TO DISCUSS

- ➤ Why didn't Jayden want to admit her thoughts to Mrs. Jones?

- ➤ Did Jayden make the right choice by admitting what was bothering her?

- ➤ What do you do when you have negative thoughts about yourself?

THOUGHTS TO CONSIDER

Jayden's negative thoughts caused her to lose her confidence and become insecure about who she is and the job that God had called her to do. Oftentimes, when we feel things such as insecurity, doubt, or fear we pull away from people that are attempting to help us. It is important that we share those thoughts and feelings with a parent even though it might be hard to do. We should never allow those negative thoughts or feelings to determine how we live our lives.

In order to replace negative thoughts with God's truth, you first need to know His Word. It is important that you constantly remind yourself of what God says, so that you will remember it in times of need. When you feel unloved, you will remember: I am a child of God, and I am loved by God. When you don't feel important, you will remember: God wonderfully made me, and I am precious to Him. When you are disappointed that you are not as good at a task as someone else, you will remember: I have unique gifts from God that were given to me the moment I was born.

PRAYER

Dear heavenly Father,

Thank You for believing good things about me. When I think negative things about myself, please remind me that You don't want me to think that way. Please help me to remember how You see me. Thank You for sending Jesus to redeem me from my mistakes. In Jesus' name, I pray. Amen.

DAY 49

DAILY CONFESSION

God wonderfully made me, and I am precious[1] to Him. I am a child of God, and I am loved by Him. My birth was not an accident. I have unique gifts from God that were given to me the moment I was born. I am a wise person because God gives me skillful wisdom, knowledge, and understanding. I am always saved by God. He always has a plan to rescue me from trouble, even when I make wrong choices. I am forgiven because Jesus washed away my sin when he died on the cross.

MEMORY SCRIPTURE

In him we have redemption through his blood, the forgiveness of sins, in accordance with the riches of God's grace... Ephesians 1:7

JAYDEN'S STORY CONTINUED

What am I doing here? I am just a kid, and I am going to mess something up during the event tonight, Jayden thought as she walked into her church. Realizing that negative thoughts were once again clouding her mind, she stopped in her tracks. She was alone in the quiet hallway, so she closed her eyes, and she thought, *I will not allow these negative thoughts to ruin my evening. God, please help me to remember what You think about me.* Her mind cleared. *God wonderfully made me, and I am precious to Him. I am a child of God and loved by God. My birth was not an accident. I have unique gifts from God that were given to me the moment I was born. I may only be a 12 year old girl, but God has a good plan for my life, and He can use me to do His work.* She opened her eyes and began walking with confidence. She thought, *I better get moving. I have a job to do!* Jayden busied herself with the rest of the volunteers as they prepared the church for the evening activities.

Just as Jayden finished drawing the third hopscotch court, she was greeted by Mrs. Jones. "Hi Jayden! Thanks for arriving early to help set up for the game night."

"No problem," smiled Jayden. "By the way, I took your advice about replacing my negative thoughts with what God believes about me. It really helped."

"I am happy to hear that, Jayden. I wish I could tell you that you will never have another negative thought, but I can't. However, I can promise you that replacing those thoughts with God's thoughts will always help you. God will never let you down," encouraged Mrs. Jones.

Their attention was turned to the kids that were starting to enter the church. Jayden announced, "I am going to help direct the kids to the game stations."

"Thank you," answered Mrs. Jones as they both walked towards their separate tasks.

Jayden happily greeted several of the kids as they entered the room. After several minutes, she noticed a young girl at the hopscotch station crying. Concerned for the young girl, Jayden ran to her and compassionately asked, "Hey, why are you so sad?"

"Max said I messed up the game! I don't even know how to play hopscotch. I don't want to play anything, because I mess everything up," she sobbed.

Jayden encouraged the little girl, "You might have messed up this time, but that doesn't mean that you mess *everything* up. Do you know what God thinks about you?" The little girl had a puzzled expression and shook her head. "God loves you very much. He wonderfully made you, and you are precious to Him. He will give you wisdom, to include wisdom on how to play games. Did you know He wants you to have fun tonight?"

"He does?" she asked.

Jayden smiled at the little girl, grabbed her hand and said, "Yes, He does! C'mon, I am going to teach you how to play this game, and I think you are really going to like it!"

QUESTIONS TO DISCUSS

- ➢ How did Jayden overcome her negative thoughts?
- ➢ Did Jayden's conflict help her to understand the little girl's sadness?
- ➢ How was Jayden's conflict similar to the little girl's conflict?

THOUGHTS TO CONSIDER

When Jayden recognized that her thoughts did not agree with God's thoughts, she put into practice the advice from Mrs. Jones. She replaced the negative thoughts with the words of God. Jayden immediately felt better. If you will follow Jayden's example by recognizing a negative thought and replacing it with the words of God, you will probably see an immediate change in your mind and feelings. Is this always true? No! Sometimes you might have to practice this many times before you begin to see a change. Whatever you do, don't give up your hope in God! The Bible is true, and God is faithful to do what He says.

God is good, and He never causes bad things to happen in your life. Even so, when bad things do happen in your life, He always works to cause something good to result from the bad circumstances. God did not cause Jayden to forget to check the microphones, and He certainly did not cause her to think negative thoughts about herself. As soon as Jayden encountered trouble, God immediately went to work and caused several good things to happen. First, He gave Addison and Mrs. Jones wisdom to help Jayden overcome her problem. Second, He gave her mom wisdom so that she could guide Jayden to pray. Third, He gave Jayden wisdom and strength so that she could overcome her problem. Finally, He gave Jayden an opportunity to share her new wisdom with someone facing a similar problem.

PRAYER

Dear heavenly Father,

Thank You for loving everything about me. Please help me to trust the Bible to include what You think about me and your love for me. Thank You for always helping me. In Jesus' name, I pray. Amen.

MESSAGE FROM MELISSA

Intentionally pursuing God makes you a true superhero in my book. Overloaded to-do-lists and constantly changing schedules complicates the life of even the most proficient time managers. Whether you blasted through this devotional without skipping a beat or you barely cracked open the book on most days, pat yourself on the back for intentionally endeavoring to help your child spend quality time with the Creator. If this devotional has blessed you or your child in any way, please take a moment to rate this book on Amazon and visit www.applyingfaith.com. Thank you!

May the Lord bless you and protect you. May the Lord smile on you and be gracious to you. May the Lord show you His favor and give you His peace. Numbers 6:24-26

BELIEVER'S PRAYER

Has your child prayed the Believer's Prayer? If not, there is no better person to lead them than you, and there is no better time than now. It is truly very simple. Here is what you need to do:

1. Ask your child the following questions:

    ➢ Do you believe that Jesus is the son of God?

    ➢ Do you believe that Jesus died on the cross and was raised from the dead three days later?

    ➢ Do you want to trust and obey Jesus?

2. If your child answered yes to all three of these questions, then your child is ready to pray the Believer's Prayer. Lead your child in the following:

       Dear heavenly Father,

       I believe that Jesus is your son. I believe that Jesus died and You raised Him from the dead three days later. I ask that Jesus come into my heart, and I will trust and obey Him. The Bible tells me that whoever calls on God will be saved.[2] Thank You for hearing my prayer and saving me![3] In Jesus' name, I pray. Amen.

ENDNOTES

[1] Since you are precious and honored in my sight, and because I love you...
Isaiah 43:4.

He will rescue them from oppression and violence, for precious is their
blood in his sight. Psalm 72:14

[2] And everyone who calls on the name of the Lord will be saved. Acts 2:21

[3] If you declare with your mouth, "Jesus is Lord," and believe in your heart
that God raised him from the dead, you will be saved. For it is
with your heart that you believe and are justified, and it is with
your mouth that you profess your faith and are saved. Romans
10:9-10

www.ingramcontent.com/pod-product-compliance
Lightning Source LLC
LaVergne TN
LVHW011155080426
835508LV00007B/414